The Dissolution of Yugoslavia: The History of the Y Political Problems that Led to Yugoslavia's Demise

By Charles River Editors

The flag of Yugoslavia

About Charles River Editors

Charles River Editors is a boutique digital publishing company, specializing in bringing history back to life with educational and engaging books on a wide range of topics. Keep up to date with our new and free offerings with this 5 second sign up on our weekly mailing list, and visit Our Kindle Author Page to see other recently published Kindle titles.

We make these books for you and always want to know our readers' opinions, so we encourage you to leave reviews and look forward to publishing new and exciting titles each week.

Introduction

Marshal Tito and Eleanor Roosevelt

Yugoslavia

"No country of people's democracy has so many nationalities as this country has. Only in Czechoslovakia do there exist two kindred nationalities, while in some of the other countries there are only minorities. Consequently in these countries of people's democracy there has been no need to settle such serious problems as we have had to settle here. With them the road to socialism is less complicated than is the case here. With them the basic factor is the class issue, with us it is both the nationalities and the class issue. The reason why we were able to settle the nationalities question so thoroughly is to be found in the fact that it had begun to be settled in a revolutionary way in the course of the Liberation War, in which all the nationalities in the country participated, in which every national group made its contribution to the general effort of liberation from the occupier according to its capabilities. Neither the Macedonians nor any other national group which until then had been oppressed obtained their national liberation by decree. They fought for their national liberation with rifle in hand. The role of the Communist Party lay in the first place in the fact that it led that struggle, which was a guarantee that after the war the national question would be settled decisively in the way the communists had conceived long before the war and during the war. The role of the Communist Party in this respect today, in the phase of building socialism, lies in making the positive national factors a stimulus to, not a brake on, the development of socialism in our country. The role of the Communist Party today lies in the necessity for keeping a sharp lookout to see that national chauvinism does not appear and develop among any of the nationalities. The Communist Party must always endeavour, and does endeavour, to ensure that all the negative phenomena of nationalism disappear and that people are educated in the spirit of internationalism." - Tito

Yugoslavia was arguably one of the most unusual geopolitical creations of the 20th century. The Yugoslav state had never existed in any historical sense, and the ties that bound together its constituent peoples were tenuous at best. Although nominally all "Slavs," the country was an amalgamation of languages, alphabets, cultures, religions and traditions, which ensured its short existence was littered with splits, conflicts, and shocking violence. In a sense, it's somewhat surprising that it lasted as long as it did.

In the wake of World War I, as the political boundaries of Europe and the Middle East were redrawn, the Kingdom of Yugoslavia, initially known as the Kingdom of Serbs, Croats and Slovenes, came into existence with a monarch as its head of state. Confirmed at the 1919 Versailles Conference, the "first" Yugoslavia was a particularly fragile enterprise, and there was almost constant tension between the majority Serbs and the other Yugoslav nationalities, especially the Croats. As a result, the Kingdom was a land of political assassinations, underground terrorist organizations, and ethnic animosities. In 1929, King Alexander I suspended democracy and ruled as a dictator until he himself was assassinated in 1934.

The Kingdom of Yugoslavia was particularly vulnerable to the forces that engulfed the rest of Europe at the end of the 1930s, including fascism and communism. When the Axis forces attacked in 1941, the country quickly capitulated and was dismembered by the Nazis and their allies. A separate Croatian state was formed, led by Ante Pavelić, who committed some of the worst crimes and human rights abuses of the war. The Balkan region was virtually emptied of its Jewish population, victims of the Nazi Holocaust.

From the beginning, fascism was opposed by two major groups in the region, the monarchist Chetniks and the communist Partisans. The latter, led by Josip Broz Tito and backed by the democratic powers, emerged in the dominant position at the end of the war. The World War II era produced many leaders of titanic determination, men whose strengths and weaknesses left an extraordinary imprint on historical affairs, and the struggle between massively divergent ideologies catapulted some individuals unexpectedly onto the world stage. Marshal Tito was undoubtedly one of these figures. Originally a machinist, Tito leveraged his success in the Communist Party of Yugoslavia (CPY) and a number of extraordinary strokes of luck into dictatorial rule over Yugoslavia for a span of 35 years. World War II proved the watershed that enabled him to secure control of the country, leading an ever more powerful army of communist partisans against both the Germans and other Yugoslav factions. During the war, SS leader Heinrich Himmler himself begrudgingly stated, "He has really earned his title of Marshal. When we catch him we shall kill him at once...but I wish we had a dozen Titos in Germany, men who were leaders and had such resolution and good nerves, that, even though they were forever encircled, they would never give in.

During his reign, Tito managed to quash the intense national feelings of the diverse groups making up the Yugoslavian population, and he did so through several methods. He managed to successfully play the two superpower rivals, the United States and Soviet Union, off against each other during the Cold War, and in doing so, he maintained a considerable amount of independence from both, even as he additionally received foreign aid to keep his regime afloat. All the while he remained defiant, once penning a legendary letter to Joseph Stalin warning the Soviet dictator, "To Joseph Stalin: Stop sending people to kill me! We've already captured five of them, one of them with a bomb and another with a rifle... If you don't stop sending killers, I'll send a very fast working one to Moscow and I certainly won't have to send another."

Never afraid to use political murder when expedient, yet simultaneously outgoing and good-humored to those around him, Tito created a unique and unusual state between the Western democracies and the Eastern Bloc. However, after Tito's death in 1980, Yugoslavia quickly moved into its final phase. Without Tito, the country was weakened by other structural factors such as an economic crisis, rising debt and chronically low productivity, and Yugoslavia slumped into a decade of economic stagnation in the 1980s. Without growing prosperity, the constituent republics and its peoples were more susceptible to a different, more chauvinistic brand of politics.

Internal issues plagued the country in its final years and Tito had tinkered with Yugoslavia's constitution on several occasions. His final attempt, in 1974, saw the partial separation of Kosovo – crucial in the Serb national story – from the rest of Serbia. A number of reasons led to the rising Serb nationalist sentiment after Tito's death, but Kosovo was a central aspect. Yugoslavia required far-sighted, magnanimous leaders to avoid internecine disputes, but none were available, or at least in positions of power in the 1980s. In Croatia, Franjo Tudjman – a long time Croat nationalist – emerged as the republic's leader, and Slobodan Milošević rose to prominence in the middle of the decade and, despite apparently being a career communist, positioned himself as "defender of the Serbs." He began ousting his rivals and installing sympathetic underlings into leadership positions in Kosovo, Vojvodina, and Montenegro, essentially giving him a majority bloc at the federal level.

Depending on the source, many authors have focused on different catalysts for Yugoslavia's demise, but Vesna Drapac may have succinctly summed the situation up when he wrote that by the end, the state "lacked a reason to exist."[1] There is certainly something in this sentiment, but the disintegration came at an enormous cost.

[1] Vesna Drapac, Constructing Yugoslavia: A Transnational History, (Basingstoke: Palgrave Macmillan, 2010), p. 257.

The Dissolution of Yugoslavia: The History of the Yugoslav Wars and the Political Problems that Led to Yugoslavia's Demise examines how the multicultural nation broke apart in the 1980s and 1990s. Along with pictures of important people and places, you will learn about the Yugoslave Wars like never before.

The Dissolution of Yugoslavia: The History of the Yugoslav Wars and the Political Problems that Led to Yugoslavia's Demise

About Charles River Editors

Introduction

The Balkans' Different Ethnic Identities

The Formation of Yugoslavia

Immediate Instability

Tito's Yugoslavia

The 1980s

Yugoslavia's Dissolution

The Bosnian War

The Bitter End

Online Resources

Bibliography

Free Books by Charles River Editors

Discounted Books by Charles River Editors

The Balkans' Different Ethnic Identities

"If you humble yourself too much, you will get trampled on." – Ancient Serbian proverb

Though the Turkish persecution of the Serbians under the Ottoman Empire is a part of Serbian history that is often swept under the rug, their descendants never forgot the seemingly endless trials of their ancestors. The Muslim Turkish rulers not only set out to erase the Serbian social elite, they were determined to sever the Orthodox Christian roots its population desperately clung to. Those who could afford it fled to neighboring nations for refuge, while the rest were ejected from their rightful lands, left with no choice but to set up camp in "hostile mountains."

The homes and properties of all Orthodox Christian Serbians were promptly confiscated by Turkish authorities, and the bulk of the people were unwillingly tethered to a system of serfdom under their foreign masters, otherwise known as the "*giours.*" Their new subjects, the Serbian masses, were derogatorily referred to as the "*rayah,*" meaning "the herd." Even worse were the suffocating laws that singled out the Christian Serbs. They were only to possess mules, leaving horses, camels, and other "superior" means of travel for Turkish and Muslim use. On that note, they were never to ride a mule in the presence of a Muslim, nor could they own houses or other property that would outshine a Turkish abode. Fantastic churches and *rayah* buildings were torn down in droves, and what was left of them in pitiful conditions at best, their church bells rusting over from neglect. Needless to say, erecting new ones was out of the question. The *Rayah* were forbidden from burying their dead in broad daylight, nor could they utter the name of Christ in the presence of a Muslim.

Turkish sultans kidnapped generations of Christian Serbian children – some say up to 5 million – to equip their slave-fueled Janissary armies under a system called the *"devsirme."* Authorities whipped these boys into shape, and exploiting their Stockholm syndromes, implanted in their young minds a ride-or-die loyalty for their captors. Many Ottomans abused their privileged positions, the worst of them employing the *jus primae noctis*, or the "right of the first night." Plainly put, Turkish men were granted first dibs on Serbian servant women on their wedding nights, a humiliating practice that carried on until the 19th century. The list of injustices seemed to stretch on for miles.

There existed a door that guaranteed one access to a much brighter future, but like most entries, it came attached with a price of admission. A Serbian had to formally renounce their Christian faiths and embrace the Ottoman brand of Islam. Only then would the rights of a "full citizen" be bestowed upon them. Many struggled at the crossroads. Some, fretting over the futures of their loved ones, made the tentative step over the line, whereas most refused to budge, digging their heels into the ground.

The early 1800s brought about the first wave of Serbian insurgencies. The Serbians rejoiced as the revolutionary leader, a ferocious man known only as Karađorđe ("Black George"), took matters into his own hands and beheaded the quartet of Janissaries previously heading Serbia, relieving the people from the crush of their heels. By December 1806, Karađorđe and his troops had seized Belgrade, soon to become its capital.

Karađorđe

For the next 7 years, the Serbians ran their own ship, giving them their first, albeit fleeting, taste of freedom. Karađorđe was named the Grand Vožd of Serbia, and in 1808, a constitution of Serbia's own was published. Not only did Christian churches appear again, a string of Serbian schools were established in Belgrade, one of which eventually blossomed into a prestigious university.

By October 1813, however, Turkish soldiers swarmed into Serbia once more, replanting their flags in Belgrade in short order. As the story goes, Turkish authorities, infuriated by the Serbians' insubordination, allowed their soldiers to slay any Serbian over the age of 15 and enslave as many maidens and children as they could get their hands on for a period of two weeks. Up to 1,800 Serbian slaves were sold in a day.

Rather than submit to the Ottomans, the Serbian hunger for independence only grew more powerful. While much of their physical culture had been destroyed by their oppressors, subsisting only on a few epic poems about Serbian victories on the battlefield and the like, the Serbian spirit had not lost its character. The Serbian community not only held strong to their Orthodox Christian beliefs and distinctive cultural traits, their increasing exposure to foreign democracies continued to fan the flames of their patriotism.

Merchants who journeyed to Habsburg-operated Hungary with stacks of plump, acorn-fed pork in their wagons were some of the first to dip their toes into the light at the end of the tunnel. This was a place that treated Christians – albeit German Catholics – with due respect, and it appeared to accept the Orthodox Serbian neighbors with little to no hesitation. A few Serbians even held posts in Hungarian administrative offices and enlisted for the Austrian side during the Austro-Turkish War. It was here that they picked up on Hungarian military tactics and organizational skills that allowed them to secure their seven year spell of independence. They also found a father figure of sorts in Russia, for this modern "Slavic and Orthodox country" had become a formidable threat to the Ottomans.

More Serbians began to chase trade and educational opportunities beyond the border, and as such, they explored unfamiliar, but groundbreaking schools of thought in regards to philosophy, law, politics, and societal values shaped by rationalist and romanticist ideals. Serbian scholars left and right attempted to revitalize the local culture. Dositej Obradovic, a traveling monk, not only translated a number of foreign texts, he spun together a series of dictionaries and grammatical textbooks penned in the modern Serbian tongue. Another Enlightenment-era wordsmith, Vuk Karadzic, churned out collections of epic poetry dedicated to Serbian identity, many of its values sympathizing with the peasant communities.

By 1867, the Principality of Serbia would be awarded some semblance of independence, but the 1878 Congress of Berlin cemented the Austrian administration's position behind the scenes. Many, particularly the peasant and newly-enlightened masses, saw this not only as a stall in progress – to subject themselves to outside authority would mean taking a tremendous step backwards. It would not be long before their suspicions were realized, for Serbian conservatives, many of them supposedly puppets of the Austrians, began to drive a rift between the local patrician and plebeian classes. Only Serbian elites were inducted to civil office and awarded privileges the peasant classes were robbed of, for the plebeians were deemed too uneducated and incompetent to handle governmental affairs. What was more, the voices of the peasantry were often silenced; those who spoke out against the government were immediately tossed behind bars on the charge of public disobedience.

Belgrade pulsed with the cries of liberal university students who sided with the plebeians, many lambasting the conservatives for their "draconian legislation and hollow...corrupt system of administration." The discontent among the masses continued to swell, spawning an epidemic of overzealous, fanatical nationalism. This phenomenon was anything but lost on one notorious underground syndicate known as the "Black Hand," which would capitalize on these feelings of frustration and resentment to push for the creation of a Greater Serbia. So potent was their vision that they were willing to go to any extreme to secure it.

In order to fully understand the implications and motivation for the Black Hand's actions, it's necessary to understand the situation in Serbia and the Balkans as a whole, and why a small region whose chief importance in the previous centuries had been as a battleground for the great powers to control access to Europe became responsible for the outbreak of World War I. Three years after Archduke Franz Ferdinand's birth, in 1878, the Great Powers signed the Treaty of Berlin, a document intended to pacify the Balkans, where the Ottoman Empire had been forced to use brutal force to suppress rebellion on more than one recent occasion. Among other clauses, the Treaty empowered the Austro-Hungarian Empire to take nominal charge of the Bosnia District of the Ottoman Empire, although it officially remained Turkish territory. At the same time, the Treaty also acknowledged the sovereignty of the Principality (later the Kingdom) of Serbia, under the aegis of King Milan Obrenovic, whose family was closely connected to Emperor Franz Joseph's and was well-liked at court. This diplomatic connection helped ensure stability within a notoriously volatile region; administrative power passing to a European power with a Christian government and a long-term vested interest in the East helped quell much of the turmoil to which the Balkans had been subject to under Ottoman rule, while Serbia provided a useful and friendly bulwark to calm any unrest which might occur.

The tension in the Balkans was symptomatic of what was occurring in Europe as a whole. In the briefest of terms, by 1900 there existed in Europe an interconnected series of alliances, treaties and pacts, both overt and secret, that were intended to maintain the balance of power and the status quo on the mainland, the likes of which had never been seen before. The purpose of this web of alliances was ostensibly to ensure peace, but in reality it meant that an aggressive power could wage small-scale wars with virtual impunity thanks to the looming threat of a full-scale escalation on the European mainland, as had occurred during the Schleiswig-Holstein Question and the Franco-Prussian War (both conflicts started by what was now Germany).

The first of these alliances emerged in the wake of the Napoleonic Wars with the creation of the Holy Alliance, a "triumvirate" of Austria, Russia and Prussia. 60 years later, Otto von Bismarck, perhaps the greatest politician of his age (and certainly the most effective champion of the Prussian cause), created the *dreikaiserbund*, the League of the Three Caesars, a re-affirmation of the previous alliance renegotiated to include Germany. Fittingly, this alliance fell apart over the Balkans, as Russia and Austria-Hungary were at odds over how to administer and exert influence across the region. Thus, in 1879, Germany and Austria-Hungary dropped Russia as a partner to form the Dual Alliance, and three years later, Austria set aside its differences with Italy, which had recently fought two viciously contested wars of independence against Austria to achieve sovereignty. Together, these three nations formed the Triple Alliance.

Bismarck

Things held together (albeit in an extremely fragile fashion) until roughly 1890, shortly after the ascension to the throne of Germany of Kaiser Wilhelm II. Wilhelm was concerned about the vast and shadowy power still wielded by Bismarck, so he compelled Bismarck to resign out of fear that he would undermine the legitimacy and power of the German monarchy by being the de facto ruler. This was a legitimate fear given that the diplomatic circles of Europe still contacted Bismarck over matters of international policy thanks to their decades-long familiarity with him. What Wilhelm failed to take into account was just how much Bismarck had wielded his personality, ruthlessness, personal magnetism and sheer diplomatic brilliance to keep Germany safe and ensure its constant expansion despite the minefield of European politics. With Bismarck gone, the fragile, informal diplomatic ties he had maintained disintegrated, and in 1890 the Kaiser committed a serious political blunder by refusing to renew the Re-Insurance Treaty, which guaranteed mutual non-aggression between Russia and Germany. Russia then went on to sign the Franco-Russian Alliance with France in 1902, effectively hemming in Germany between two largely hostile powers. France also signed a treaty with Britain, the Entente Cordiale, and in 1907 Britain involved itself further in European affairs by signing the Anglo-Russian Convention. These were not formal alliances, but for simplicity's sake, this complex Anglo-Russian-French arrangement is usually referred to as the Triple Entente. While there were no formal guarantees that Britain would intervene if either France or Russia were attacked or went to war, they certainly strengthened the possibility that this would occur.

Matters in Europe were further complicated by the massive escalation of an arms race. In the wake of the Franco-Prussian War of 1871, Germany had established itself as the dominant power in Europe, and German industrial output had grown by orders of magnitude. By the dawn of the 20th century, Germany was even competing with the mighty Royal Navy for domain over the world's oceans, an impressive output for a country that had never truly made naval power a priority. The *Kaiserliche Marine*, with its modern destroyers, worried the British so much that in 1906 they launched HMS *Dreadnought*, the most powerful battleship of its time. This race for technological supremacy was as much saber-rattling as it was a genuine policy to ensure sufficiently modern equipment in fear of an attack by another European great power, but regardless, military spending almost doubled among most of the powerful nations. Moreover, virtually all nations adopted new breech-loading bolt-action rifles to go along with new artillery pieces, heavy and super-heavy mortars and railway guns, machine guns, grenades, poison gas shells, and a host of other instruments of destruction. As a result, weapons were becoming deadlier and more powerful just as nations like Germany and Italy were following burgeoning imperialistic agendas, and just as the British and French sought to prevent their expansion.

Nevertheless, the creation of Yugoslavia long predates the Cold War. It was a creature of the post-World War One settlement and of the Versailles Conference.[2] The country consistently lacked popular legitimacy, including during its first phase. The various component nationalities were suspicious of one another, particularly the smaller nations towards the majority Serbs. It is worth considering how the state of Yugoslavia came about at all. The answer lies in the particular confluence of geopolitics – the collapse of two huge empires, Austro-Hungary and the Ottomans – as well as a small but committed group of proponents. Crucially, during the First World War between 1914 and 1918, the Allied Great Powers - Britain, France and the United States – all quiesced to the foundation of Yugoslavia, or the Kingdom of Serbs, Croats and Slovenes.

Turmoil Before World War I

The Balkan area has historically been one of the world's most combustible regions. Home to several national groups and at a crossroads of Europe, Asia and the Middle East, the Balkans have exerted an outsized role on world affairs. Infamously, the assassination of Austrian

---

[2] Dejan Djokić, *Pašić & Trumbić. The Kingdom of Serbs, Croats and Slovenes*. (Haus Publishing, 2010)

Archduke Franz Ferdinand by a Serb nationalist, Gavrilo Princip, caused the dominoes to fall, leading to the First World War.

The Balkans, however, had been flammable long before Princip's bullets murdered the Austrian monarch-in-waiting. A number of countries had attempted to expand their borders within the Balkan region, and many of these had been supported by larger continental powers, such as Russia, Britain, France, Austria, Germany, and Italy. The main cause of this instability was the decline of empire in the Balkans; the Ottoman Empire had held sway over the southeast section of the Balkans since the 15th century, while the Austrian Habsburgs were dominant in the northwest of the region. Both empires moved into relative decline in the 19th century, albeit in different ways. The Ottoman territories were slowly lost to other encroaching forces, while the Austrians (and then Austro-Hungarians) actually expanded until the First World War. This turned out to be a case of "imperial overstretch," and as the two hegemons weakened, a number of political spaces opened up. The wake of World War I would produce a nation made up of Serbs, Croats, Bosnians, Slovenes, Macedonians, and Montenegrins. These nationalities, however, would not prove satisfactory for many in the new country, and others would later emerge, most notably the Kosovan Albanians and Bosniaks.

In addition to the nationalities that would be part of Yugoslavia, the Balkans was home to a number of other identities, ethnicities, and traditions, and the Greeks, Bulgarians, Romanians, Albanians and Turks would all play a role in the development of Yugoslavia as well.

As mentioned earlier, the Serbs had shown themselves to be potent adversaries in the Balkan region and prized themselves as warriors. Notions of a Serb-nation focused on the 1389 "Battle of Kosovo," on the "Field of Blackbirds," where the Ottomans had defeated a Serb army but nevertheless gave Serbia a sense of identity in a hostile region. Kosovo also became an integral part of any notion of a Serb state. As a predominantly Christian Orthodox people, Serbia also gained fraternal support from co-religionists, most notably Russia.

Croatia was the second largest of the Yugoslav nations. Croats were Catholic and saw themselves as more inherently part of European "civilization" compared to the other Yugoslav nationalities, though it should be noted that this sentiment was shared by most of the Slavic ethnicities. The region that incorporates modern Croatia was part of the Austrian Habsburg Empire for several centuries and gained some autonomy in 1868. Croatian nationalism had grown during the century, and a number of groups were agitating for full independence during the First World War.

Bosnia, meanwhile, was a more complicated area. Home to large minorities of self-described ethnic Serbs and Croats, the majority of Bosnians were Muslim, sometimes (later) known as Bosnian Muslims or Bosniaks. Bosnians had lived in the territory for centuries but enjoyed some preferential treatment under the Islamic Ottoman Empire. Nevertheless, a specific version of Bosnian nationalism grew during the 19th century, and the country – known as Bosnia and

Herzegovina – was occupied by Austria-Hungary from 1878 and annexed in 1908.

Slovenia, wedged between Austria, Italy, and Croatia at the foot of the Alps, was another Catholic area, but with its own unique language. Most of the other nationalities spoke a version of Serbo-Croat, even if the alphabets they used varied. Slovenia was part of the Austro-Hungarian Empire, but it also experienced a surge in nationalist sentiment, particularly after the continent-wide revolutions of 1848.[3]

Macedonians lived in the region bordering today's Greece, which was still part of the Ottoman Empire in the early 19th century, and Macedonia also bordered Albania and Bulgaria. Macedonia had particular links with the latter, including linguistically and culturally, and the territory included a significant minority of ethnic Albanians. Macedonia proved to have one of the most potent national movements of the era, manifesting itself notoriously as the Macedonian Revolutionary Organization (MRO), which, although relatively small in number, played a role in weakening the Ottoman Empire.

Montenegrins were the last piece of the ethnic jigsaw puzzle. Set on the Adriatic Sea, Montenegro had come under the control of the Ottomans, Habsburgs, and Venetians at various times. The tiny country gained principality status in 1852 and then full independence from the Ottomans in 1878. Traditionally, Montenegro had been close to Serbia and fought on the same side during the First World War, but it was occupied by Austrian forces between 1916-1918.

As the Austro-Hungarian and Ottoman Empires teetered in the late 19th century, Balkan countries all sought to expand their borders.[4] In their own ways, each Balkan nation had what was known as a "Big Idea" (from the Greek "Megali Idea"), a project to maximize its boundaries to the furthest possible point and incorporate various historical claims. The list of conflicts is long and perplexing, and it included the war between the Russians and the Ottomans that culminated in the 1878 Congress of Berlin, presided over by German Chancellor Otto von Bismarck. The year 1878 saw an increase in Serbia's territory, independence for other countries from the Ottomans, and the Austrian occupation of Bosnia and Herzegovina. The Treaty of San Stefano confirmed the territorial changes, in particular the enlargement of Bulgaria.

From the Congress of Berlin until 1914, Balkan countries would be locked into competition, making the region a cauldron of violence and instability.[5] In addition, the Great Powers felt compelled to involve themselves in the region. It appeared that Russia backed change and the dismemberment of the Ottoman Empire, whereas Britain seemed to support the status quo encapsulated by the existing situation.[6]

---

[3] Oto Luthar, *The Land Between: A History of Slovenia* (Frankfurt am Main: Peter Lang, 2008), p. 280.

[4] Mark Mazower, *The Balkans: From the End of Byzantium to the Present Day* (London: Phoenix, 2001), p. 126.

[5] Misha Glenny, *The Balkans 1804-2012: Nationalism, War and the Great Powers* (London: Granta, 2012), pp. 133-134.

[6] Tom Gallagher, *Outcast Europe: The Balkans, 1789-1989: From the Ottomans to Milošević*, (London: Routledge,

Along with the conflicts between empires and states, a number of events and movements within the Balkan countries themselves would affect the foundation of Yugoslavia. In June 1903, a group of Serb army plotters, led by Captain Dragutin Dimitrijević (otherwise known as Aspis), assassinated the pro-Austrian Serb King Alexander Obrenović and his wife in Belgrade, as well the Prime Minister.[7] The crown then passed to the Karađorđević family and King Pete I. The new monarch gave a free hand over government policy to the military while being more sympathetic to Russia. As a result, Serb policy developed in a more hostile fashion towards the Austro-Hungarian Empire.[8] Intrigue in Serbia, however, was not over. Aspis later founded the secret Black Hand organization of Serb nationalists in 1911. The Black Hand would gain historical infamy with its role in starting the First World War and Gavrilo Princip was its notorious member. Macedonian underground groups were also active during the first years of the 20th century and launched an uprising in 1903, put down by 40,000 Ottoman troops.

2001), p. 31.

[7] Richard J. Evans, The Pursuit of Power: Europe 1815-1914 (London: Penguin, 2017), p. 691.

[8] Ibid, p. 691.

Драгутин Т. Димитријевић-Апис

Dragutin Dimitrijević

Aleksandar

Meanwhile, in the Ottoman Empire, a group of disgruntled military units and underground organizations, revolted in 1908. Known as the "Young Turk Revolution," the uprising was the beginning of the end of the empire and the rise of Turkish nationalism. To its neighbors, the Young Turk revolt was proof that the Ottomans were in weakened position, and Austria's response was to formally annex Bosnia and Herzegovina.[9] It would not be long before others attempted to fill the power vacuum.

The uncertainty in the Balkan region provided impetus for all the nationalist groups as the

---

[9] Misha Glenny, *The Balkans 1804-2012: Nationalism, War and the Great Powers* (London: Granta, 2012), pp. 218-219.

empires went into terminal decline, and the situation erupted in a number of conflicts in 1912 and 1913 that became known as the Balkan Wars. Albanian tribesmen occupied Skopje (the capital of today's Republic of Macedonia), providing the spark for others to move. In October 1912, Bulgaria, Greece, Montenegro, and Serbia all commenced hostilities, attempting to expand their territory.[10] Soon it was the Serbs that occupied Skopje. Meanwhile, Greek forces occupied the ancient port city of Salonika, pushing out the Ottomans after hundreds of years.

The fighting threatened to drag in the larger powers, and consequently the British convened a peace conference. The Treaty of London was signed in May 1913 to draw the map of the region, essentially without the Ottomans.[11] Soon afterwards, however, fighting resumed and Bulgaria gained land, confirmed in the Treaties of Bucharest and Constantinople.[12]

The wars had been relatively short in duration, but the modern military techniques had proven destructive, killing 200,000 men on all sides. As historian Richard J. Evans noted, "These wars were a portent of things to come."[13] The Balkan Wars also created a certain picture of the region in the minds of Western Europeans, especially as reports from the period described Balkan "barbarism" and particularism in the savagery undertaken by combatants.[14] It was a reputation that lasted the entire 20th century, and it was so powerful that outside powers tried to justify intervention in the Balkan conflicts of 1912-1913 through Christian "Just War Thinking," invoking a duty to prevent savagery.[15]

The Formation of Yugoslavia

There were very few people within the Balkans who backed a Yugoslav state before 1918.[16] The concept of a union of the different nationalities in the region was the brainchild of a limited group of thinkers, which ensured Yugoslavia was essentially a top-down project. The two key architects of the state were Nikola Pašić, a Serb, and Ante Trumbić, a Croat.[17] The pair set up the "Yugoslav National Committee" in Paris in 1915, and this culminated in the July 1917 "Corfu Declaration," which set out the basis of a Yugoslav state, or a Kingdom of Serbs, Croats and Slovenes as it was then known.[18] France and Britain became early supporters of the Yugoslav project, seeing it as a potential bulwark against previous foes. Some, but by no means all British and French policy-makers believed that a Southern Slav state could prevent further instability in the region, which had been so instrumental in causing the war in the first place.

---

[10] Richard J. Evans, The Pursuit of Power: Europe 1815-1914 (London: Penguin, 2017), p. 693.

[11] Ibid, p. 695.

[12] Ibid, p. 695.

[13] Ibid, p. 697.

[14] Eugene Michail, 'Western Attitudes to War in the Balkans and the Shifting Meanings of Violence, 1912-1991', *Journal of Contemporary History*, (47:219, 2012), pp. 219-241)), p. 220.

[15] Ibid, p. 222.

[16] Mark Mazower, *The Balkans: From the End of Byzantium to the Present Day* (London: Phoenix, 2001), p. 114.

[17] Robert Gerwarth, *The Vanquished: Why the First World War Failed to End, 1917-1923* (London: Allen Lane, 2016), p. 189.

[18] Ibid, p. 197.

Pašić

Nikola Pašić was already in his late 60s by the start of World War I and had a long career in Serbian politics behind him. Pašić was Prime Minister in 1914 when the Austrians presented him with the "July Ultimatum," and although he accepted most of its demands, Vienna concluded that the Serb government and the "Black Hand" were one and the same. In exile during the war, Pašić became the leading Serb negotiator for the idea of a unified Slav state. During his long career, Pašić was most adept at gaining and accumulating power. Coupled with the instincts of Serb nationalism, he may have seen the Yugoslav project as a means of extending its influence.[19]

Although he may not have been personally enthusiastic about the idea, he was faithful to the wishes of the Serbian regent, Alexander, who was. Pašić also believed a number of assurances

---

[19] Misha Glenny, *The Balkans 1804-2012: Nationalism, War and the Great Powers* (London: Granta, 2012), p. 369.

had been made to the Croats and Slovenes during the war, alluding to a security alliance that needed to be honored in forming a unified state.

   Croat leader Ante Trumbić, born in 1864, may have been even more fervent in desiring a unified nation. During the war, Croatia was forced to fight with the Austrians, but Trumbić, leading the London-based Yugoslav National Committee, lobbied the Allied Powers to accept the idea of Yugoslavia after the end of the conflict.[20] On July 20, 1917, the Corfu Declaration was signed and laid the foundation for Trumbić and Pašić's state. Shortly after the end of the First World War, on December 1, 1918, a Kingdom of Serbs, Croats and Slovenes was declared. Several days earlier, Serbia had formed a separate union with its ally Montenegro.[21] The Great Powers left the final settling of the state's borders for the imminent Versailles Conference, to be held near Paris.

Trumbić

Even before the state's foundation, tensions began to simmer between the different

[20] David Owen, *Balkan Odyssey* (London: Indigo, 1996), p. 7.
[21] Dejan Djokic, 'Versailles and Yugoslavia: ninety years on', *Open Democracy*, 26 June 2009, https://www.opendemocracy.net/article/versailles and yugoslavia ninety years on

nationalities. The Croats and Slovenes saw the benefits of a united Slav state in terms of security; having been occupied for centuries by the Austrians, they were now wary of an expansionist Italy, which, having been on the side of the victors during the First World War, now sought territorial recompense. In particular, the Italians were making a claim on parts of the Dalmatian Coast in Croatia. The pooling of resources could buttress Croatia and Slovenia against outside threats, and ultimately this was crucial in the acceptance of a unified state under Serbian leadership.[22]

Nevertheless, a key principle was left unresolved between Pašić and Trumbić that would repeatedly come back to haunt Yugoslavia. Trumbić and the Croats believed they were signing up for a loose federation in which the component republics, namely Croatia, would have significant autonomy. Pašić and the Serbs, however, favored a unitary and more centralized state, naturally led by the majority Serbs. This tension led to several constitutions, a number of revolts, and the collapse of the country altogether generations later.[23]

In modern history books, the Treaty of Versailles looms large. Ostensibly called to formalize the end of the war, the prominent decision-makers at Versailles sought to punish the aggressors in the war and to stabilize Europe, in order to prevent further conflagration. The conference has been interpreted in many ways, but it is most widely remembered today as punishing Germany so harshly that it inadvertently led to World War II.

Versailles also brought about the creation of a number of new states, including Yugoslavia. The three major players at Versailles were French Prime Minister Georges Clemenceau, British Prime Minister David Lloyd George, and American President Woodrow Wilson. President Wilson came to Versailles with a separate, although clearly related set of priorities. Having issued his famous "Fourteen Points" for ending the war in January 1918, Wilson put more emphasis on democratic accountability and self-determination. At Versailles, this meant that new states were formed while border territories were given the option, through plebiscites, of choosing whether to join one state or another.[24]

This also meant that numerous delegations arrived at Versailles putting forward their cases for national sovereignty. For Yugoslavia, Nikola Pašić and Ante Trumbić were there, as well as nationalists from the countries that would constitute the unified state. These included an obscure Croatian nationalist by the name of Ante Pavelić, who was opposed to the Yugoslav idea, believing it to be a "Greater Serbia" project.[25] Pavelić would become one of the most notorious

---

[22] Mark Mazower, *The Balkans: From the End of Byzantium to the Present Day* (London: Phoenix, 2001), p. 114, David Owen, *Balkan Odyssey* (London: Indigo, 1996), p. 7.

[23] Robert Gerwarth, *The Vanquished: Why the First World War Failed to End, 1917-1923* (London: Allen Lane, 2016), p. 198.

[24] Godfrey Hodgson, *People's Century: From the dawn of the century to the eve of the millennium* (Godalming: BBC Books, 1998), p. 80.

[25] Robert Gerwarth, *The Vanquished: Why the First World War Failed to End, 1917-1923* (London: Allen Lane, 2016), p. 189.

figures in the state's history.

Pavelić

One of the key problems for the architects of the post-war world in Versailles was that when Wilson's ideas came into contact with reality, sovereignty and self-determination for some was not inclusive for others. It would prove impossible to draw borders containing discreet national groups, and this was evident within the multinational Kingdom of Serbs, Croats and Slovenes. Despite the liberal, progressive rhetoric at Versailles, the new states clearly included minorities that either did not want to live in the new arrangement or would be persecuted by the majority group.

Czechoslovakia and the Kingdom of Serbs, Croats and Slovenes were among the new states that officially came into being on June 28, 1919, five years after Gavrilo Princip had assassinated

Franz Ferdinand in Sarajevo. In Yugoslavia's case, a better way of describing Versailles was that its creation was not opposed by the Great Powers.[26] Moreover, the young state still had border disputes with Italy and Romania which remained unsettled until the 1920s.[27]

As the dust settled after Versailles, the Yugoslav delegation returned home to start the serious business of building a new state from scratch. Due to its previous domination by different empires, not to mention its different languages, cultures, and traditions, the separate republics had quite different structures. Pašić was temporarily out of power in the new state, while Trumbić was appointed foreign minister. Serbian monarch King Peter I assumed power over the new country, while his son, Alexander, wielded influence behind the scenes as Regent.

Alexander I

The early formation of Yugoslavia was quite different from the federal version that emerged

[26] Dejan Djokic, 'Versailles and Yugoslavia: ninety years on', *Open Democracy*, 26 June 2009,
    https://www.opendemocracy.net/article/versailles-and-yugoslavia-ninety-years-on
[27] Ibid.

after 1945. It contained six customs areas, five currencies, four rail networks, three banking systems, and initially two seats of government in Belgrade and Zagreb.[28] The region was overwhelmingly an agricultural economy, as approximately 75% of the population still worked on the land.[29] The state was split into a number of provinces, which broadly speaking can ᴸ as Slovenia, Croatia, Serbia, Bosnia, and Montenegro.

The new state, despite being a multiethnic formulation, paid little attention to a number of other nationalities present in the region in 1918. These included ethnic Germans, Greeks, Turks, Hungarians, Romanians, and Albanians.[30] Although the politics of the Kingdom bore some semblance to its European contemporaries - for instance a Social Democratic party existed, as well as the Democratic Party - there were numerous ethnically based parties, such as the Serbian Radicals, the Croatian Peasant Party, and the Slovenian People's Party. The Croat Peasants, dominated by Stjepan Radić, were initially proponents of an agrarian socialism and Croat autonomy, while the Democrats were the major voices for a centralized state.

Radić

[28] David Owen, *Balkan Odyssey* (London: Indigo, 1996), p. 7.
[29] Misha Glenny, *The Balkans 1804-2012: Nationalism, War and the Great Powers* (London: Granta, 2012), p. 396.
[30] David Owen, *Balkan Odyssey* (London: Indigo, 1996), p. 7.

Immediate Instability

One of the first challenges for the new state was to pass a constitution. The document barely achieved parliamentary consent on June 28, 1921 after having been proposed the previous year. In fact, it achieved only a simple majority, as opposed to the 60% stipulated in the Corfu Declaration.[31] It became known as the "Vidovdan Constitution," as it shared the date of the famous remembrance of Serb national identity.

A new administrative structure was set out in the document, with 33 new Oblasts (provinces) essentially forming a unitary, Serb-led, centralized monarchy. Nationalists in the smaller non-Serb areas were outraged. For Croats and Slovenes, this was a betrayal of the agreements made during the First World War. Support for the new state weakened in its peripheral regions throughout the next two decades, and almost immediately, peasant groups violently opposed the 1921 constitution.[32] Indeed, the battle over the constitution paralyzed politics over the first half of the 1920s, with the main Croat nationalist leaders refusing to participate.

The dominant figures in the first phase of Yugoslavia were politicians such as Nikola Pašić and the Karađorđević monarchy. The Karađorđević family had been locked in a battle for influence in Serbia throughout the 19th century with the Obrenović family. The former was pro-Russian, while the latter was pro-Austrian, and each wanted to reduce the influence of the opposing power.

The 1903 coup that murdered the Obrenović king appeared to have settled the Serbian monarchy question, and King Peter I had been on the throne as Serbia gone through the successes and failures of World War I and the formation of the Kingdom of Serbs, Croats and Slovenes. Peter I now projected more Serb influence than had existed, in the Serbian nationalists' eyes, for hundreds of years.

It was Peter I's son, Alexander, however, who was the more committed supporter of a unified Yugoslav state of Southern Slavs. Alexander, then 32 years old, became king in August 1921 following the death of his father, and he would play a pivotal role in the historical development of Yugoslavia over the next decade. King Alexander I's erratic rule proved antagonistic to the ethnic minorities within the state, particularly the Croats, and this rivalry overshadowed the early years of the country. Croat nationalists were not the only minority to sour over the idea of Yugoslavia, as some of the most potent challenges to the new state were Macedonian underground groups.

The IMRO (Internal Macedonian Revolutionary Organization, the successor of the MRO) had already made its mark on Balkan history thanks to its campaign of improvized violence and subversion at the turn of the century. In a unified Yugoslavia, the Macedonians were clearly

---

[31] Misha Glenny, *The Balkans 1804-2012: Nationalism, War and the Great Powers* (London: Granta, 2012), p. 403.
[32] Mark Mazower, *The Balkans: From the End of Byzantium to the Present Day* (London: Phoenix, 2001), p. 114.

subjugated behind other nationalities, and the IMRO and other Macedonia underground groups such as the Macedonian Federative Organization (MFO) renewed their provocative activities. During the 1920s, the IMRO circulated rumours that Italy was about to invade, causing grave concern among Croats in particular.[33] The IMRO had a number of objectives, ranging from gaining separate autonomy within a Balkan Federation to being incorporated into the Bulgarian state.

The Kingdom of Serbs, Croats and Slovenes ostensibly managed to settle its boundary questions with the Treaty of Rapallo in November 1920. Located south of Genoa, the Rapallo document was signed by the Yugoslavs and Italy, settling the status of Dalmatia and Istria within Croatia. For the Croats, however, this was a bitter pill to swallow, as the Treaty proposed independent sovereignty over a number of cities in Istria and Dalmatia, including Rijeka (known as Fiume to Italians).[34] Nikola Pašić had disturbed the Croats in the Yugoslav delegation during the wartime negotiations with the Allied Powers through his potential willingness to sign over Croat and Slovene land to the Italians in return for land favored by Serb nationalists in Macedonia and Albania.[35] Indeed, as Prime Minister, Nikola Pašić formally signed these territories over to Benito Mussolini in January 1924, much to the dismay of Croats. Meanwhile the newly formed countries in the region – Yugoslavia, Czechoslovakia and Romania – formed the so-called "Little Entente," an alliance to improve their respective positions against the former imperial powers, in 1920.

Pašić had returned to office in 1921 and became the dominant figure in the first years of the nation. Although Yugoslavia was nominally democratic, these institutions never took root in the first decades of the state's existence.[36] Much was made of this in later years, but clearly democracy in the Balkans was relatively novel. Moreover, if voters simply supported parties of their own nationality, democracy was likely to be extremely difficult. The only idea that truly cut across the different ethnicities was socialism, and this would not gain broad support for awhile. In the 1920s, political parties found it difficult to appeal to several part of the nation.

Croat separatists such as Radić came in behind the Belgrade authorities for a time in the mid-1920s. The Croatian leader had been jailed in January 1925 on charges that his party had broken a 1920 law, the Obznana Decree, which had been initially designed to suppress the Communist Party. Shortly afterwards, however, Radić stunned his opponents and supporters alike by throwing his weight behind the Vidovdan Constitution. In fact, the Croatian Peasant Party leader came to an agreement with King Alexander I due to the threat posed to Croatian integrity by Mussolini's fascist Italy. The king realized he needed his country's two biggest parties to come to terms with each other if he was to achieve stability. Therefore, Radić instructed his nephew to

---

[33] Nada Boskovska, *Yugoslavia and Macedonia Before Tito: Between Repression and Integration* (London: IB Tauris, 2016)

[34] Misha Glenny, *The Balkans 1804-2012: Nationalism, War and the Great Powers* (London: Granta, 2012), p. 377.

[35] Ibid, pp. 369, 377.

[36] David Owen, *Balkan Odyssey* (London: Indigo, 1996), p. 7.

make a statement to the Belgrade parliament: "The Vidovdan Constitution exists here today de facto, this is a political fact of life, with the Karadjordjević (Karađorđević) dynasty as the head of the state. This is a fact which we accept unconditionally and with which we agree…Although it may look as though we have made concessions to our brothers, those brothers are the Serbian people and represent our joint future together."[37]

Radić was released from prison shortly after the declaration, and the development was a major breakthrough in the already fractious history of Yugoslavia. King Alexander I brokered a coalition agreement between the Serbian Radicals and Radić's Croatian Peasant Party, and for a time the country seemed to be moving into a new phase of peace and prosperity. The economies of major cities such as Zagreb and Belgrade appeared to boom.

The truce only lasted, however, until the next round of discord threatened to overwhelm the fragile state. Pašić resigned in 1926 due to a corruption scandal, and his son Rade was implicated in a number of graft allegations that became a point of constant criticism from the Croatian Peasant Party.[38]

Relations between the Serb Radicals and Croatian Peasant Party deteriorated after Pašić, a flawed politician but one who could at least claim to represent some continuity, resigned. The parliament, known as the Skupština, became home to almost daily shouting matches, intimidations, and squabbles which threatened to turn violent. Stjepan Radić himself had been threatened on several occasions by other parliamentarians.

On June 19, 1928, a member of the Serb Radicals, Puniša Račić, pulled out a revolver in the parliament and shot three Croatian Peasant Party MPs, including Radić. The Croat leader initially appeared to recover, but he died on August 8 of that year.[39] The assassinations caused outrage across the country, especially in Croatia. The government attempted to struggle on, but disputes only grew, and coalitions proved impossible to form.

On January 6, 1929, King Alexander I suspended the democracy and effectively seized power for himself as part of a monarchical dictatorship. Alexander renamed the Kingdom of Serbs, Croats and Slovenes in October 1929 to the more familiar Yugoslavia, loosely translated as Land of the Southern Slavs.

The king remained obsessed with the "Croat Question," and how to pacify the demands of Croat separatists while maintaining the integrity of the Yugoslav project. It is worth noting that the other nationalities did not always support Croat claims of Serb dominance. Indeed, the Slovene People's Party and the (Bosnian) Yugoslav Muslim Organization often supported Belgrade in the disputes with Zagreb in the 1920s.[40]

---

[37] Misha Glenny, *The Balkans 1804-2012: Nationalism, War and the Great Powers* (London: Granta, 2012), p. 405.
[38] Ibid, p. 407.
[39] Ibid, pp. 408-412.

Nonetheless, Croat nationalists were certainly developing greater animus to the Yugoslav state by the end of the decade. The controversy over the Vidovdan Constitution, territorial concessions to Italy, and the 1928 assassinations had provided much fuel to the separatist fire. The feeling held by Croat nationalists was that Yugoslavia was a Greater Serbian project that was either indifferent, or at worst hostile to Croat sentiments. Radić's funeral – acting as a locus of Croatian nationalism and grievance - was attended by hundreds of thousands, and the red and white chequered flag, subsequently synonymous with the Ustaše terrorist group, was brandished at the funeral for the first time.

Another Croat nationalist, Ante Pavelić, fled Yugoslavia in 1929, having contacted the IMRO. Pavelić had already established an underground Croat group, known as the Ustaše, from the acronym UHRO (Croatian Revolutionary Organization). The Ustaše attracted emigres who were living in exile across Europe, particularly Austria, and started a campaign of violence and assassinations within Yugoslavia. Pavelić was tried and sentenced to death in Yugoslavia, but by this point he had fled into exile in Mussolini's Italy.[41] This suited Mussolini, who had come to power in 1922 and saw the possibility of splitting Yugoslavia and gaining greater regional influence for Italy.

Many more Yugoslavs would become sympathetic to groups such as the Ustaše and the IMRO after October 1929 and the Wall Street Crash. Although the crash took place in the United States, it impacted virtually every economy that participated in the global trading system. King Alexander I responded to the crisis in a number of ways, strengthening central (that is to say Serb) control over the economy. The national minorities in Yugoslavia believed that they suffered more economic pain than the majority Serbs, therefore intensifying the rivalries and animosities that had built up in the 1920s. The country was straining under the limits of the Gold Standard, and the level of its foreign trade declined.

King Alexander I had also reorganized the administrative structure of his country shortly after its name change to Yugoslavia. 33 Oblasts became nine new regions, or *banovinas*, and in 1931 he signed a new constitution that put executive power officially in the hands of the monarch. Democracy in Yugoslavia had been officially extinguished.

Alexander formed a separate autocratic tool for his decrees, called the "Court for the Protection of the State," which stifled any opposition to the king. The Court quickly arrested the two most prominent opposition politicians, Vladko Maček and Svetozar Pribićević. Maček had become leader of the Croatian Peasant Party after Stjepan Radić's assassination in 1928, and as a leading opponent of the king, he was jailed in 1933 for treason. Svetozar Pribićević, on the other hand, was a Serb from Croatia who strongly supported the idea of Yugoslavia. Pribićević had been a Democrat before setting up a splinter party, but, having changed his mind about a centralizing

[40] Misha Glenny, *The Balkans 1804-2012: Nationalism, War and the Great Powers* (London: Granta, 2012), p. 408.
[41] Ibid, p. 430.

approach, formed a political partnership with Croat nationalists such as Radić. He was jailed in 1929 but released in 1931 due to poor health. Pribićević became a leading critic of Alexander's dictatorship from exile in Paris before his death in 1936.

Extrajudicial killings were also prevalent. In February 1931, a leading Croatian intellectual who opposed Yugoslavia, Milan Šufflay, was murdered outside his home by members of the royalist Young Yugoslavia group. The murder provoked an international outcry.

Ante Pavelić, in exile in Italy, took more extreme positions during the 1930s.[42] His vision for an independent Croat state incorporated more and more of Yugoslavia. Pavelić was developing his own "Big Idea" of Croatia, as many Croats lived in Bosnia and Herzegovina as well as regions of Serbia. The Ustaše leader appealed to both Croat emigres and, most predominantly, peasants. In this respect he filled the space of the Croatian Peasant Party led by Radić and then Maček. In 1933, in *Principles of the Ustaše Movement*, Pavelić wrote, "The peasantry is not just the base and source of our life but alone contains the essence of the Croatian people and is, as such, the executive of all state power in the Croatian state." As a result, Pavelić could recruit ordinary Croats to his cause.

At the same time, he also kept links with other underground groups and it was to them he turned to initiate his most incendiary move against the Yugoslav state to date. Pavelić eventually contacted the Macedonian IMRO to plot the assassination of King Alexander I. Having settled on a plan, the IMRO assassins, led by Vlado Chernozemski and backed up by Croats, traveled through Hungary to Switzerland to France, where the king was due to attend a state visit as part of his country's Little Entente agreement. On October 9, 1934, King Alexander I arrived in Marseille, France and began his visit accompanied by the French Foreign Minister through the city in an open car. Chernozemski appeared from the crowd and shot the king twice, killing him.

Tito's Yugoslavia

"Comrade Khrushchev often repeats that Socialism cannot be built with American wheat. I think it can be done by anyone who knows how to do it, while a person who doesn't know how to do it cannot build Socialism even with his own wheat. Khrushchev says we live on charity received from the imperialist countries … What moral right have those who attack us to rebuke us about American aid or credits when Khruschev himself has just tried to conclude an economic agreement with America?" - Tito

Following the end of World War II, the Yugoslav Army (formerly the Partisans) executed tens of thousands of their adversaries, including former Chetniks, Ustashe, and others. Mihailovic himself fell into Yugoslavian hands, and the Yugoslavs executed him in 1946. This, of course, also had the fringe benefit of eliminating many people who might have objected strenuously to

---

[42] Misha Glenny, *The Balkans 1804-2012: Nationalism, War and the Great Powers* (London: Granta, 2012), p. 433.

the establishment of a communist state.

Tito, riding a wave of triumph and military glory, brazenly engineered the takeover of the nation by his party, the People's Front, in late 1945. Though Yugoslavia held elections on November 27th, 1945, Tito loaded the ballot-boxes in his favor by declaring that large lists of people could not vote due to supposed collaboration with the Germans. In fact, the list consisted mostly of people believed to be anti-communist, with no reference in most cases to any real connection with the Germans.

Since he had effectively declared that only Partisans and their known supporters could vote, Tito engineered a 90% victory for the People's Front. With his party now immovably in power, Tito abolished the monarchy just two days after the general election, and King Petar II Karadjordjevic fled to the United States, where he died in 1970.

King Petar II

Initially, Yugoslavia showed itself to be a ferociously Marxist state, with a secret police, purges of dissenters, numerous arrests, and suppression of religion in the name of communist atheism. Catholic Archbishop Alois Stepinac received a prison sentence of 16 years for alleged

Ustashe activity, though the communists steadily reduced his sentence later. The Archbishop's imprisonment caused the Pope to excommunicate Tito.

Tito's communist party also took over most of the major industries immediately. Tito launched a Five-Year Plan for rapid economic expansion. The CPY expropriated huge amounts of private property. Any factory that worked even a single day during the war years received the label of a "collaborating" business and fell to automatic expropriation by the state. Next, Tito's government seized all property and factories belonging to foreigners, including Yugoslav allies such as the British and Soviets.

The First Five-Year Plan rolled an incredible 27% of Yugoslavia's gross national product back into economic development, 92% of it industrial. This outdid the scope of even the Soviet Union's Five-Year Plans, and caused considerable hardship to large sectors of the populace as production of food and consumer goods dropped to build up a stock of capital goods (manufacturing machinery).

Initially, Tito's slightly unique take on Marxism won praise from the Soviets, as a 1947 article indicated: "The concrete embodiment of the ideas of Marxism regarding the unity of the working class with the majority of working people [...] has been most consistently developed in Yugoslavia where the People's Front unites almost seven million people [...] The People's Front [...] is a social-political organization of the people in which the working class, headed by the Communist Party, plays a leading role." (Swain, 2011, 90).

However, Yugoslavia soon split with Stalin and the USSR due to Tito's maverick leadership. Tito, in a bid to assist a communist revolution in Greece, effectively invaded Albanian territory to protect Greek communist bases there, without first consulting or even informing either Stalin or Albania's leader Enver Hoxha. Though the Soviets eventually outwardly accepted this action, they began pressuring Tito to add Yugoslavia to a planned Balkan Federation. The Federation, under Soviet control, would effectively reduce all of the member countries, Yugoslavia included, to the helpless provinces of what might be called a "greater Soviet empire." An exchange of letters followed, in which Stalin claimed that the Yugoslavian success in World War II stemmed entirely from the Red Army. In fact, this represented a complete falsehood; the Yugoslavian Partisans largely won the war in their own country independently, while most of what aid they did receive came from the British, not the Soviets, whose support always appeared lukewarm.

The communist Cominform convened in Bucharest on June 28th, 1948 and expelled Yugoslavia from its fold. Though it issued an invitation to Tito and his top lieutenants to attend, Tito refused to travel there, noting "if we have to be killed, we'll be killed on our own soil." (Swain, 2011, 96). That was a clear insight, given Stalin's long history of summoning people to areas he controlled in order to have them killed.

Thus, for several months, Yugoslavia existed in a sort of vacuum, with the Soviet Union looming over it in wrath. Tito already looked towards the Americans, perplexed by the entire affair, to save him from the USSR, declaring, "The Americans are not fools. They won't let the Russians reach the Adriatic." (Banac, 1988, 137). This essentially encapsulated Tito's foreign and domestic policy for the rest of his reign as Yugoslavia's dictatorial president – maintaining a species of communist state while relying on tacit Western support to keep the Soviet juggernaut at bay. Edvard Kardelj, Yugoslavia's Foreign Minister, provided a succinct summary of how his nation could maintain itself as an unaligned state between the two vast power blocs of the 20th century, the free world to the west and the communist world to the east, by leveraging the "tendency among the imperialists to exploit the contradictions between the socialist states, very much in the same way as we wish to exploit the internal contradictions of the imperialist system." (Banac, 1988, 138),

Kardelj

The U.S. and England cautiously adopted a "wedge strategy" towards Yugoslavia, supporting it in order to keep it out of the Soviet sphere of influence and put up a roadblock in the way of Stalin's European ambitions. Tito accordingly ceased giving aid to the Greek communist organizations, paid back U.S. Lend-Lease aid, and remunerated English and American people whose property in Yugoslavia had suffered expropriation. Still, the Americans naturally remained cautious of Tito's and Yugoslavia's intentions. They also could not quite decide how to deal with a country that housed a repressive, dictatorial Marxist regime, yet showed strong signs of nationalism and showed itself willing to defy the still-ascendant power of Moscow. As George Frost Kennan, an influential Cold War political strategist, said of Yugoslavia, a "new factor of fundamental and profound significance has been introduced into the world communist movement by the demonstration that the Kremlin can be successfully defied by one of its own minions (Lees, 1997, 54). By 1955, the US government had given Tito more than $1.2 billion in combined economic and military aid. The English also provided assistance, though on a lesser scale due to their waning power.

Tito's regime gradually moved away from a purely communist approach as the pragmatic demands of survival placed effectiveness ahead of ideology. The Yugoslavians tried a three-year trial period of collective farms, or SRZs, after which they asked the peasants if they wished to stay or leave. Flooded with gigantic numbers of requests to leave, Tito and his cabinet decided to return 1.5 million acres of agricultural land to individual peasant family ownership in 1952. Collective farming vanished in most areas by 1953, with a few notable exceptions.

At around the same time, the Yugoslavian state developed one of its other unique characteristics, the principle of self-management. Under this scheme, many factories worked not at the direction of a cumbersome and dangerous central bureaucracy as in the case of the Soviet Union, but by "workers' councils" elected and staffed by the laborers at the factory themselves.

Showing considerable acuity, Tito declared in 1950 that the USSR actually represented a counterrevolutionary state. Stalin, he said, operated the entire Soviet Union as a gigantic capitalist monopoly. His method, he claimed, placed the means of production into the hands of those Marx intended: the workers themselves. When the West invented the term "Titoism" to describe Tito's rule in Yugoslavia, by contrast, Tito claimed that he represented the true Marxist and that Stalin was the "heretic:" "It is simply that we have added nothing to Marxist-Leninist doctrine. [...] Should 'Titoism' become an ideological line, we would become revisionist; we would have renounced Marxism. We are Marxists, I am a Marxist and therefore I cannot be a 'Titoist.' Stalin is the revisionist: it is he who has wandered from the Marxist road. 'Titoism' as a doctrine does not exist." (Dedijer, 1953, 432).

This, of course, represented something of a semantic dodge, unlike Tito's insightful remark that Soviet communism resembled a gigantic monopolistic corporation. Yugoslavia under Tito matched no other state on the planet. Soon, the workers' councils at the factories received permission to make investments and other business decisions, using the funds their efforts earned, independent of state interference, provided that "ownership" remained divided equally between everyone who worked at the factory and decisions occurred by vote rather than "board of directors" fiat.

On the personal scale, Tito's success with women continued. The Yugoslavian leader met a nurse, Jovanka Budisavljevic, after a gall bladder operation and married her in 1951. Jovanka remained married to Tito for the next 29 years until he died, though their relationship broke down to some degree several years before his death. Jovanka lived until 2013, witnessing both the entirety of Tito's reign and the significant events of the post-Tito era.

Dragan Zebeljan's picture of Jovanka

Stalin's death in 1953 while Tito was visiting Britain represented a major change in Soviet leadership. Tito attempted rapprochement with the Soviet Union, only to be largely rebuffed by new Soviet leader Nikita Khrushchev. However, in 1955, Khrushchev visited Belgrade, and, after reaching something of an understanding with Tito, both men signed the Belgrade Declaration. This promulgated an agreement of mutual non-interference, and Khrushchev canceled all of Yugoslavia's debts upon his return to the Soviet Union.

Khrushchev

Tito felt safe enough to visit Moscow in 1956, and Khrushchev and Tito continued their diplomatic dance for the rest of the decade, but Yugoslavia – in the person of its leader – steadfastly refused any agreement that would reduce the country's independence. Tito continued playing the East and West off against each other in order to keep his own country essentially safe from major external interference throughout the 1950s.

Tito continued to enjoy the high life as he aged, living in superbly furnished castles, supplying himself with every luxury, and continuing to pursue women besides his wife Jovanka. However, he also continued to pay attention to running his unusual state and addressing problems as they arose. In the early 1960s, the self-management program ran into problems due to the difficulties of allotting investment funds. Officials managed to take over the distribution of these funds, compromising the independence of many self-managed factories. This led to the production of unnecessary or substandard goods as the officials pursued their own agendas without reference to market demand.

Tito in 1961

At the same time, consumer demand burgeoned as the economy recovered and the self-management program produced genuinely effective economic activity. Tito waffled for some time, apparently trying to coordinate his efforts with Khrushchev, but the latter's fall removed the likelihood of any cooperation between the Yugoslavian and Soviet economies that would not leave Moscow with the whip hand and strip Tito of his independence.

At the Eighth Party Congress in 1965, Tito increased the amount of money that self-managed factories could retain for investment to 70%, up from the current 30%, thus improving the economic position of the workers and attempting to reduce the power of the officials to interfere in the economy's functioning. The bureaucracy naturally resisted this, wishing to retain its control over investment and thus economic planning and activity.

Tito returned to a measure of centralization in the final decade of his life. Though self-management remained a key portion of the Yugoslavian economy, the 1974 Constitution made the state's structure much more hierarchal, giving Tito the power to resist change and try to keep his creation as an unchanging structure for the rest of his life. The Constitution also named Tito president for life in its first article.

Tito continued to enjoy his extravagant lifestyle during the final decade of his life. However, he no longer had the energy of youth and his infinitely complex system began to ossify without his constant tinkering and guidance. The dissident Milovan Djilas noted, "In the late 1960s, Yugoslavia had another chance, the most promising if also the most uncertain, at democratization … [but by] the early 1970s Tito more firmly than ever held back the movement for change; he forced creative social, national and individual potentialities to revert to the withered ideals of his youth." (Swain, 2011, 189). Nevertheless, Yugoslavia enjoyed nearly first-world standards of living and a unique system of "self-management" that did not match either communist or capitalist designs. Regardless of its flaws and Tito's human failings, Josip Broz had created a relatively prosperous state that remained separate from the problems of other Cold War countries east or west.

Tito died in early 1980 at 88 years of age, killed by gangrene caused by a leg amputation following arterial blockage. An enormous number of heads of state, including 31 presidents and four kings, attended the funeral of the Croatian machinist who had witnessed and participated in the most tumultuous events of the 20ᵗʰ century.

The 1980s

Tito's death was certain to create a power vacuum in Yugoslavia. He had attempted to stabilize the country's politics with a new constitution in 1974 that set out a collective, rotating leadership, but he also failed to appoint a political successor. The settlement worked for a few years, but several shocks, political and economic, caused fault lines to appear, and these issues worsened as politicians started to agitate nationalist bases in the 1980s. The end of the Cold War further weakened Yugoslavia, leading the country to the brink of disaster.

In fact, as soon as Tito died in 1980, nationalist émigré groups were hailing, predicting or calling for the demise of Yugoslavia.[43] Several countries were home to significant expatriate groups, particularly the Croat organizations. The first actual post-Tito unrest, however, took

---

[43] John R. Lampe, *Yugoslavia as History: Twice there was a country* (Cambridge: Cambridge University Press, 2000), p. 299.

place in Kosovo in 1981. Ethnic Albanian groups, particularly students, protested against a range of issues, including history teaching and using the Albanian language. The subsequent riots disturbed the elites in Belgrade, as well as the minority Serbs in Kosovo.[44] The province's place in Serb history gave it particular significance as the birthplace of a conscious Serb nation, following their battle with the invading Ottomans in 1389. That Serbs may be losing their privileged position in the province, or even being threatened or persecuted by ethnic Albanians, led to acute sensitivity. A trend missing during the years of the socialist Federation was Serb nationalism. When it returned, the edifices holding Yugoslavia together began to crumble.

It was something altogether less emotive that first debilitated Yugoslavia in the post-Tito years: the economy. It may appear as if the state only faltered after Tito's death, but the 1980s were in fact the fruition of many of the dictator's policies. Tito had allowed Yugoslavia to live beyond its means for years and acquired a liking for foreign debt. He was somewhat different from his peers because he effectively shared income with his people. However, when Western banks had to contend with high interest rates in the late 1970s and early 1980s, pressure was inevitably passed on to debtors, including Yugoslavia. By 1983, the country was in serious economic trouble.

The impact of Yugoslavia's economic frailty was not immediately obvious. The country successfully hosted the 1984 Winter Olympic Games in Sarajevo, glorifying in its mantra of brotherhood and multinational and multi-religious harmony.[45] By this time, however, the Federation lacked any substantial figures. In many ways, in the mid-1980s, it resembled other Central European and Eastern European countries, as party functionaries in bland suits talked about unlikely production targets and factory output. This political impotence and latent economic problems – high inflation, low productivity, high debt and need for hard currency – would culminate in the horrors of the 1990s' conflicts when exploited by nationalists. Initially, however, the nationalist impulse was one of self-preservation by weak communist politicians. The most notable – or infamous - example of a career communist who turned to nationalism during the decade was Slobodan Milošević.

---

[44] Carole Rogel, *The Breakup of Yugoslavia and its Aftermath* (London: Greenwood Press, 2004), p. 17.
[45] Zlatko Jovanovic, 'The 1984 Sarajevo Winter Olympics and Identity-Formation in Late Socialist Sarajevo', *The International Journal of the History of Sport* (34:9, 2017, pp. 767-782).

Milošević

Slobodan Milošević was born in 1941 in Serbia, then occupied by the Nazis during the Second World War. He became active in the Yugoslav Communist Party youth section during the 1960s while he was at university in Belgrade. At this time, he became acquainted with Ivan Stambolić, whose uncle Petar Stambolić was a key member of the Serbian communist executive.

Starting in local politics, Milošević worked his way up to prominence in Serbian politics by the 1980s. Yugoslavia may have been nominally an egalitarian socialist state, but connections were often important in career progression. Milošević had essentially been mentored by Ivan Stambolić and, using his uncle, began to scale the ladder of Yugoslav communism. Interestingly, in light of later events, Stambolić was considered a "liberal" within the spectrum of Yugoslav politics. By the time of his death in 2006, Milošević had made a reputation with his own particularly virulent form of nationalism, far from the communism of fraternity and brotherhood he embraced in his youth.

By 1984, he had been elevated to a leadership position in Belgrade, and in 1986 Milošević was voted President of the Serbian League of Communists. The structures of Yugoslav politics were complex and multi-layered, but essentially each republic had its own parliament and leadership which then appointed a delegate to the rotating central committee. Thus, by 1986, Milošević was in a position of some influence in Serb politics, the biggest of the Yugoslav republics, but as he moved into power, the direction of Serb society was taking a radical shift. Since the 1930s, it had been accepted that Serb nationalism would be lethal to the Yugoslav project, so for 50 years Tito and his successors had worked to satisfy the various republics and nationalities without allowing Serbs to dominate the Federation. This was, of course, difficult since Serbia was the most populous component part of Yugoslavia. This fragile, but successful, bargain lasted until the mid-1980s, when a number of Serb academics attempted to revise, or revisit, the country's history.

In 1986, the notorious SANU (translated as the Serbian Academy of Sciences) memorandum was published. The document, written by a number of academics and thinkers, aired several long-standing, suppressed Serb grievances.[46] It claimed that Edvard Kardelj (identified as a "Slovene") and Tito (a "Slovene" and a "Croat") had colluded in an attempt to keep the Serbs in a position of relative weakness in Yugoslavia. The document cited the position of Kosovo and its decoupling from Serbia in the 1974 constitution, a situation that enraged Serb national sentiment.[47] SANU berated the role of "fascist" Croats, both during the Second World War and afterwards. It revisited the old theme of centralization of power (favored by Serbs) and devolution (preferred by most of the republics). The SANU memorandum included contributions from 1960s-era Praxis intellectuals. Back in the turmoil of the 1960s, writers such as Mihailo Marković were considered reformers, but by the mid-1980s they had morphed into purveyors of virulent Serb nationalism, while Yugoslav communists, including Serbs like Ivan Stambolić, condemned the document.

It was into this background that Milošević stepped. As Serbian Communist Party chief from 1986, he certainly would have felt pressure at home to take a more assertive approach in his dealings with the other republics. He also may have seen the opportunity to garner and solidify support within Serbia by asserting nationalist claims. It was exactly this dynamic that other Yugoslav leaders had attempted to curtail as far back as the 1930s. Slobodan Milošević would eventually go down the path towards national chauvinism. The first real opportunity he had to state his nationalist credentials was over Kosovo. The Serb nation had eulogized the role the "Field of Blackbirds" had played in defining who the Serbs were, and this battlefield, in Kosovo, had been the place where Serbs had resisted Ottoman marauders all the way back in 1389. Therefore, Serb nationalists were unhappy when Tito separated Kosovo from the Serbian Yugoslav republic in his 1974 constitution.

Ironically, the document was an attempt to decentralise power in Yugoslavia and dilute the kind of nationalist agitation seen during the Croatian Spring, which lasted from 1968-1971. By the 1980s, Kosovo was inhabited by a majority (90%) of ethnic Albanians and a minority (approximately 10%) of Serbs. The former had demonstrated in 1981, demanding greater recognition of the Albanian language and historical tradition in education. The authorities had

---

[46] Laura Silber and Allan Little, *The Death of Yugoslavia* (London: Penguin, 1995), p. 31; 'SANU Memorandum', http://control.gutenberg.org/articles/SANU_Memorandum, (accessed 7 January 2016)
[47] Carole Rogel, *The Breakup of Yugoslavia and its Aftermath* (London: Greenwood Press, 2004), pp. 16-17.

cracked down severely on these demonstrations, but the episode made clear that the Kosovo issues were likely to come up again at a later date.

In 1987, it was the turn of the Serbs in Kosovo to protest. Demonstrating against alleged persecution by ethnic-Albanians, the Serbs demanded action and protection from the (predominantly ethnic Albanian) police force.[48] Their calls were answered by an unlikely source: Milošević himself. The Serb President, Ivan Stambolić, decided to start a dialogue with the protestors and despatched his trusted lieutenant Milošević to Kosovo. Milošević gave an apparently impassioned plea against nationalism in Kosovo, although he initially appeared unwilling to meet with the local Serb protestors.[49] Nevertheless, after complaints from some Serbs, he agreed to meet the nationalists against the orders of Stambolić. Milošević's stance clearly changed as he decided to explicitly back the Serb nationalists, enraging Yugoslav communists across the Federation. Still in Kosovo, at a meeting with the Serbs expressing their grievances, Milošević was informed that police were beating demonstrators on the streets. Going to the scene of the alleged violence, Milošević asserted, "No one shall dare beat you again!" Broadcast across state television that evening, Milošević became, almost by accident, the defender of the Serbs. He would cultivate this image remorselessly over the next 15 years.

[48] *The Sydney Morning Herald*, 'The rise and fall of Milošević', 12 March 2006, https://www.smh.com.au/world/the-rise-and-fall-of-Milošević-20060312-gdn4y1.html [accessed 30 October 2018]
[49] Laura Silber and Allan Little, *The Death of Yugoslavia* (London: Penguin, 1996)

Stambolić

    As Milošević sought to increase his personal power in Belgrade, Stambolić attempted to discipline Milošević, grievously concerned over Yugoslavia's fate if his deputy continued along a nationalist path. A public criticism was delivered to Milošević on state news, but this elicited a fiery response. Milošević accumulated support for his nationalist approach towards Kosovo and began to undermine Stambolić. Dragiša Pavlović, a Stambolić ally, was expelled from the Communist Party over his attitude towards Kosovo. Milošević claimed that Pavlović was soft on Albanian radicals, and Milošević also began to install loyalists into bureaucratic and advisory positions. Stambolić himself was then sacked, nominally because of a letter he had written in support of Pavlović, but in reality as a political power grab by Milošević, who succeeded him as

President of Serbia within the Yugoslav Federation. In 1988-1989, Milošević launched his so-called "anti-bureaucratic revolution" which mostly entailed removing the old guard and putting his allies into power in Vojvodina, Kosovo and Montenegro.[50] In a remarkably short space of time, Milošević had transformed himself from a dull party functionary into a Serb nationalist capable of overturning the ruling elites in the surrounding republics and accruing ever more personal power and influence.

Many books about the fall of Yugoslavia emphasize the role played by the end of the Cold War from 1989-1991, but it is important to recognise that nationalist agitation had already started to surge in Yugoslavia while the status quo in Central Europe and Eastern Europe still existed. The winds of Gorbachev's *Glasnost* – or openness – reforms blew across the communist world during this time, and a desire for greater freedom in many countries led to the overthrow of the authorities in favor of democracy and market capitalism. In Yugoslavia, the desire for greater personal autonomy seamlessly transformed into group demands, essentially national self-determination. This proved intractable since the different peoples of Yugoslavia did not live in discrete territories, and also because several of these prerogatives lent on a maximalist claim of a "Greater Croatia," a "Greater Serbia," and so on. The umbrella of socialism suppressed, for the most part, national competition in the Yugoslav Federation, which had always existed but had simply been dormant.

The growing sense of Serb domination in Yugoslavia, particularly under the aegis of Milošević, concerned the other republics. In February 1989, Slovenian leader Milan Kučan stormed out of a central committee meeting in protest. Kučan's subsequent speech defended the rights of ethnic Albanians in Kosovo, as well as his own people's autonomy, the Slovenes. Deemed inflammatory, this brought Serb protestors out onto the streets of Belgrade. Shortly afterwards, the Kosovo and Vojvodina assemblies were forced to accept constitutional changes that increased Belgrade's influence over their affairs. The short-lived period, after 1974, of greater autonomy for these two republics was over.

---

[50] John B. Allcock, *Explaining Yugoslavia* (London: Hurst & Company, 2000), p. 427.

Kučan

Milošević continued to set about consolidating his own prestige amongst the Serbs. On June 28, 1989, marking the 600th anniversary of the Battle of Kosovo, Milošević spoke to a million Serbs at a rally on the Polje battlefield itself.

Serbia was not the only Yugoslav republic to see a rise in nationalism in the 1980s. Almost across the board, nationalist sentiment grew in Yugoslavia in the decade after Tito died. The geopolitical importance of Yugoslavia declined as the West and the Soviets under Gorbachev moved towards a new détente after 1985, and there were the economic factors that eroded Yugoslav's living standards and led to a loss of faith in the federal system. One could point to structural flaws in the whole Yugoslav project, and that the country's history after 1918 had been a series of short term measures to prevent an inevitable dissolution. Nevertheless, putting all these structural factors to one side, individuals, personalities, and human agency were clearly crucial in undermining the legitimacy of socialist Yugoslavia.

First and foremost was the role played by Milošević, but other republics also played their part. In Croatia, the independently-minded group of intellectuals and agitators who rose to prominence in the Croatian Spring had been imprisoned, expelled from influential positions, or sidelined after 1971. This most likely hardened the positions of many Croat nationalists in favor of total separation from Yugoslavia. Backed by a large diaspora, particularly in the Federal

Republic of Germany, émigré groups and a considerable funding apparatus, the support network was already in place for any move towards greater autonomy for Croatia.

This was embodied in the late 1980s by Franjo Tudjman.[51] An academic and Croat cultural nationalist, Tudjman had played a key role in the 1960s' disturbances, only to have been stripped of his military rank and imprisoned on more than one occasion after the Croatian Spring. Tudjman, however, was a hugely controversial figure.[52] In the 1980s, he started to articulate the fixtures and fittings of a Croatian state. These included the flag from the Ustaše era. Having brutally committed ethnic cleansing against the Serbs during its time in power between 1941-1945, invoking the Ustaše was an inflammatory, ill-judged move. Around 12% of Croatia's population, almost 600,000 people, were ethnic Serbs, and it is not difficult to imagine how any invocation of Ustaše or the NDH (referring to the wartime, proto-fascist Independent State of Croatia) regime invoked terror and horrific memories within those communities. In response, Serb nationalist intellectuals branded Croats part of a "genocidal nation."[53]

Franjo Tudjman

Slovenia, under Milan Kučan, also moved towards autonomy in the 1980s. Feeding on sentiment across the communist world, Slovenian media called for greater democratization and respect for human rights after 1987.[54] Kučan also took his controversial stance towards Kosovo,

[51] Carole Rogel, *The Breakup of Yugoslavia and its Aftermath* (London: Greenwood Press, 2004), pp. 141-142.
[52] Carole Rogel, *The Breakup of Yugoslavia and its Aftermath* (London: Greenwood Press, 2004), p. 142.
[53] Vesna Drapac, *Constructing Yugoslavia: A Transnational History*, (Basingstoke: Palgrave Macmillan, 2010), p. 250.
[54] Viktor Meier, *Yugoslavia. A History of its Demise*, translated by Sabrina Ramet, (London: Routledge, 1995), p. 59.

which set Slovenia against the Serbs and Milošević. Slovenia was the most economically developed part of Yugoslavia and was confident it could prosper alone. It also did not share a border with Serbia, and it was relatively homogeneous ethnically (meaning it did not contain a big contingent of any other Yugoslav national minority), potentially shielding it from aggression. Once Yugoslavia began to destabilize after 1987, Slovenia saw its opportunity to break away. Kučan presented himself as a civilized democrat and the voice of reason, and clearly Slovenia's path to independence was markedly different than other republics. Thus, in his own way, Kučan played a key part in the breakup of Yugoslavia.[55]

Meanwhile, nationalist leaders had moved towards positions of influence in other parts of the Federation, such as Bosnian Serb leader Radovan Karadžić, who formed the Serb Democratic Party (SDS) in 1989.

Despite the issues, at the end of the 1980s, the fragile peace in Yugoslavia still held. It was in the economic sphere that the country appeared to be fraying.

Yugoslavia's Dissolution

Yugoslavia had straddled the line between economic frailty and independent prosperity throughout its history. Tito had managed to secure loans and financial aid from the West while retaining close relations - and therefore trade - with the communist bloc. Indeed, Yugoslavia was a rare example of a country that traded with both east and west. As a result, GDP per capita was higher in Yugoslavia than many of its contemporaries in Central Europe and Eastern Europe.

The Yugoslav model was seen by many as an acceptable socialist system, particularly considering its arrangement of local worker control over factories and production, but by the end of the 1980s, it was suffering from similar problems facing other communist countries. This was due to a combination of the world recession in the early 1980s and resulting high interest rates (and related hikes in interest payments and debt), as well as chronically low productivity, high unemployment, and emigration to other European countries.[56] In the late 1980s Yugoslavia went into a severe recession, made worse by mounting levels of debt. The IMF was called in to provide an emergency loan, and Yugoslavia had already received debt relief in 1983 and 1984, a particularly acute point in its crisis after a campaign by the American-led group "Friends of Yugoslavia."[57]

The Cold War came to a sudden climax in 1989 when the Berlin Wall fell, and the special geopolitical position of Yugoslavia was now redundant. American political scientist Francis

[55] John R. Lampe, *Yugoslavia as History. Twice there was a country.* (Cambridge: Cambridge University Press, 2000), pp. 332.

[56] Ann Lane, *Yugoslavia: When Ideals Collide*, (Basingstoke: Palgrave Macmillan, 2004), p. 158.

[57] John R. Lampe, *Yugoslavia as History. Twice there was a country.* (Cambridge: Cambridge University Press, 2000), pp. 322-323.

Fukuyama famously declared that this marked the "End of History,"[58] and that the world was now moving into a period of universal liberal democracy and market capitalism. "Washington Consensus" was coined to describe the pro-market policies pursued by the likes of the IMF and World Bank. When the Soviet Union dissolved formally in 1991, the West had seemingly triumphed in its confrontation against communism, and there would be no room for even hybrid models such as Yugoslavia's. Indeed, Yugoslavia was quickly put into this new paradigm, at least in the economic sphere. As with so many other examples during the period, a sclerotic, low growth and low productivity economy was prescribed a tough dose of austerity and liberalization in return for emergency financial assistance.

The role this "structural adjustment" program played in the onset of violence in Yugoslavia has been disputed. Some believe that it simply increased unhappiness about the status quo and heralded a more rapid disintegration of the Federation. Others believed that the IMF package was the last opportunity Yugoslavia had to reform.

The man in charge of its implementation was Ante Marković. Marković was a Bosnian Croat who had fought with Tito's Partisans during the Second World War. A communist, Marković had been President of Croatia from 1986-1988, and he became Yugoslav Prime Minister in March 1989. It is perhaps ironic then that Marković would be entrusted with implementing this most capitalist set of policies.

Despite his background, Marković was an enthusiastic economic reformer, believing the IMF package was necessary.[59] Marković tied the currency (the Dinar) to the German Mark, attempting state privatization and trade liberalization.[60] Although the initial results were uneven, Marković's reforms did appear to curb inflation and improve incomes. He was also popular and one of the last prominent pan-Yugoslav politicians of any heft. Marković was sharply critical of the leaders who had swerved towards nationalism, including Milošević, as well as Borisav Jović in Serbia and Radovan Karadžić in Bosnia and Herzegovina. Marković was both a man of the future and the past, committed not only to economic reform and a better standard of living for Yugoslavs but also rooted in the socialist view of the country as a fraternal enterprise. He was, however, unsuited to the atmosphere of Yugoslavia in its final phase, a time in which most nominally communist politicians had retreated behind nationalist shields. He desperately tried to curtail the descent into conflict in 1990 and 1991, but the politicians around him had already drawn the battle lines.

---

[58] Francis Fukuyama, 'The End of History?', *The National Interest*, No. 16 (Summer 1989), pp. 3-18.
[59] John R. Lampe, *Yugoslavia as History. Twice there was a country.* (Cambridge: Cambridge University Press, 2000), pp. 352-355.
[60] Carole Rogel, *The Breakup of Yugoslavia and its Aftermath* (London: Greenwood Press, 2004), p. 21.

Marković

The most visible moment before conflicts engulfed Yugoslavia was the 1990 Communist Party Congress, officially termed the 14th Congress of the League of Communists of Yugoslavia, which took place in Belgrade in late January 1990. The congress was called as an extraordinary meeting to discuss the various political disputes that had arisen since the previous meeting in 1986. With the Cold War quickly winding down, the different parties reverted to previous inclinations at the congress. The main dispute was between the Serbian and Slovenian delegations over the former's centralization proposals, whereas the latter wanted more autonomy for the republics. The Serbs made a number of proposals for which they could now achieve majority decisions. Milošević's manoeuvring since 1987 meant that he had, essentially, appointees and allies in charge of the Kosovo, Vojvodina, and Montenegro delegations, as well as his own Serb party. This meant Milošević commanded a bloc vote that could pass or strike down any decision he chose.

The congress dragged on for two days, full of arguments, rows, and disagreements. Milan Kučan told the Serb delegation that he needed at least the appearance of compromise over his suggestions. When this proved not to be forthcoming, the Slovenian delegation resigned and stormed out of the convention hall. Initially, the Croats were unsure of what to do and Milošević tried to persuade them to remain, knowing he could still maintain the semblance of unity even without the Slovenes. Nevertheless, after some deliberation, the Croats joined the Slovenes by leaving. The delegations from Macedonia and Bosnia and Herzegovina followed.

Whether this was all by Milošević's design or an unintended effect of his aggressive actions is hard to discern, but either way, the League was now dead.[61] The country itself was now in serious peril, decoupled as it was from the socialist ideology that had bound it together for 45

---

[61] Carole Rogel, *The Breakup of Yugoslavia and its Aftermath* (London: Greenwood Press, 2004), pp. 18-19.

years. Socialist ideology was giving way to the nationalist variety, and this movement clearly pointed to self-determination and democracy in other communist countries. The end of the Cold War and the winds of change that swept through the continent would prove more problematic in Yugoslavia, a country with so many sectarian identities.

Yugoslavia limped on throughout 1990. Without the League, the Federation was exposed even more to nationalist unrest. It was not possible for every republic to simply split from the Federation, however. Slovenia may have been mostly Slovene, but there was a significant minority of Serbs in Croatia and Kosovo. Ethnic Albanians made up a sizeable minority in Macedonia, while Bosnia and Herzegovina were almost equally divided three ways between the majority Bosnian Muslims (or Bosniaks), Bosnian Serbs, and Bosnian Croats. Independence into nationalist states unnerved the minorities, which then looked towards their majority republic for protection. This then led to ideas of Greater Croatia and Greater Serbia, which implied some territorial conquest. The number of people who identified as "Yugoslav," as opposed to their individual nationalities, was in steep decline, and only significant in number in the most ethnically-mixed republic, Bosnia and Herzegovina.[62]

Despite the issues, some political reforms took place in the country's final days. Elections were held on April 8, 1990 in each republic, the first since the 1940s. Nationalists and independence-minded parties swept the elections. Franjo Tudjman's hard-line Croatian Democratic Union (HDZ) party won in Croatia by promising to "defend" the republic from Milošević. This led to Belgrade endorsing resistance to the HDZ, or as Belgrade put it, the NDH. Croatian Serbs in Knin, in the Krajina area, led by police inspector Milan Martić, formed a militia and seized control of the region. A sizeable section of Croatia was now effectively outside the control of Tudjman's government in Zagreb. The Serb-dominated Yugoslav National Army (JNA), meanwhile, was guaranteeing the security of Serb minorities outside Serbia.

In late 1990 and early 1991 conflict had essentially begun in Krajina and was looming elsewhere in the Federation. Ante Marković was desperately trying to stabilise Yugoslavia's economy, even as his country would soon start losing its component parts.

The first to leave was Slovenia, which was never considered the most problematic of Yugoslavia's republics. One of the three key founder members in 1918 as part of the Kingdom of Serbs, Croats and Slovenes, the crucial confrontations had consistently been between Serbia and Croatia, whereas Slovenes saw themselves as more "European" than the other more "Balkan" republics. Slovenia had been part of the Austro-Hungarian Empire and therefore more a part of "civilized" Central Europe. It was also the only Catholic region in Yugoslavia besides Croatia. Slovenia's language was also different than the other republics, where Serbo-Croat dominated. Many young people in 1980s Slovenia had been behind the push towards greater democratic accountability, and Slovene President Milan Kučan had exploited the tension in Kosovo to

---

[62] Vesna Drapac, *Constructing Yugoslavia: A Transnational History*, (Basingstoke: Palgrave Macmillan, 2010), p. 248.

promote greater autonomy set apart from central (Serb) domination.

After leading the walkout of the January 1990 congress, it seemed only a matter of time before Slovenia withdrew further support from Belgrade.[63] As the rest of Europe attempted to cope with the challenges presented by the fall of the Berlin Wall, Slovenia prepared to hold a referendum on continuing membership in the Yugoslav Federation. On December 23, Slovenia held its referendum, during which 88% of voters opted for independence.

Distracted by events elsewhere in Yugoslavia, Belgrade was slow to respond. Although this did not energize nationalists in the same way it would've if Bosnia and Herzegovina or Kosovo had declared an intention to break away, the Slovene decision was actually the death knell for Yugoslavia. If it was allowed to leave unimpeded, it would surely only be a matter of time before Croatia declared independence. It was a precedent that contained its own logic.

Six months later, on June 25, 1991, Slovenia declared formal independence, and in response, the Yugoslav authorities dispatched the JNA to prevent the Slovene breakaway. Slovenia had few troops or military equipment, save the Slovene sections of the federal army, called the Slovenian Territorial Defence (TO). In a straight fight between the JNA and the Slovene forces, it would have been no contest.

A number of issues ensured that the so-called "Ten Day War" was by far the least destructive of the conflicts that gripped Yugoslavia throughout the 1990s. Most importantly, the JNA relied on the Serbs, who had to travel through Croatia and who were by no means supportive of the action. The soldiers had little incentive to fight, with the ethnicity issue neutralized in the case of Slovenia. Furthermore, there was no official force as such to fight; the TO had been organized into guerrilla fighting units, ready to engage in asymmetric warfare with 21,000 personnel.

On June 26, 1991 the Yugoslav army moved into Slovenia and came into contact with TO militias.[64] Slovene politicians immediately attempted to garner international support for their independence, and against the Yugoslav army's actions. The United Nations called for an end to the fighting, with this pressure bearing almost immediate fruit. The Yugoslavs were persuaded to come to the negotiating table, and a ceasefire was announced on July 2. Five days later, an agreement was signed on the island of Brioni, incidentally one of Tito's favorite residences, to bring the fighting to an official end. The "Brioni Accord" recognized Slovene independence and ended the short war. During the fighting, 44 Yugoslav soldiers and 18 Slovene TO troops had been killed. These casualty figures would be dwarfed by the later Balkan wars, a sign that other nationalist leaders may have thought that leaving Yugoslavia would be relatively straightforward after Slovenia.

---

[63] Carole Rogel, *The Breakup of Yugoslavia and its Aftermath* (London: Greenwood Press, 2004), pp. 18-19.

[64] John Tagliabue, 'Yugoslav Army Uses Force in Breakaway Republic; Slovenia Reports 100 Wounded or Killed', *The New York Times*, 28 June 1991, https://www.nytimes.com/1991/06/28/world/yugoslav-army-uses-force-breakaway-republic-slovenia-reports-100-wounded-killed.html, [accessed 31 October 1991]

Slovene independence was not immediately recognized by the international community, which was unsure of how to respond to nationalist agitation in Yugoslavia. It would be another six months, in January 1992 when Slovene independence was widely recognized and almost a year until it was accepted as a member of the United Nations. By this point, conflict was raging across the Federation, firstly in Croatia and then in Bosnia and Herzegovina.

The Croats had generally sided with the Slovenes as internecine politics emerged in the late 1980s. With Ljubljana exiting Yugoslavia in 1990-1991, it was clear that many Croat nationalists would also want independence. Franjo Tudjman had positioned himself as the leader of the separatists by this time, and his HDZ party had already won an electoral victory in 1990.

Croatia, however, was a far more complex issue. The main point of tension throughout Yugoslavia's history had in fact been between Serbs and Croats. This had manifested itself in the 1920s, when a Serb had assassinated the popular Croat politician Stjepan Radić. The Ustaše leader Ante Pavelić successfully plotted to murder Yugoslav King Alexander in 1934, and during the Second World War, the Nazi-backed Croat state, the NDH regime, had terrorized other Yugoslav nationalities, most significantly the Serbs. The animosity had remerged during the Croatian Spring unrest in the 1960s and 1970s. As central authority broke down in the Yugoslav Federation in the late 1980s, therefore, it did not take long for suspicion to increase between Serbs and Croats.

Separation would be difficult for Tudjman and his allies. First, Croatia contained a large Serb minority, and some Serbs had already taken matters into their own hands during the uprising in Knin in Krajina in 1990. Belgrade feared, correctly, that Croat troops would attempt to retake the enclave by force, while the Croats worried that Milošević was developing a Greater Serbia project. The Serbian strongman had by now fashioned a reputation as a defender of the Serbs, and he seemed unlikely to allow such a large number of Serbs to break away into a separate state that was potentially hostile to their interests.[65] Unlike in Slovenia, any political move would likely trigger a military response from the JNA, which by now was the only arbiter of order within the Federation. This was problematic since it was increasingly seen as a Serb-dominated army.[66]

Tension rose in early 1991 when the "Špegelj Tapes" were uncovered by Yugoslav media. They appeared to record the Croatian Defence Minister, Martin Špegelj, arranging the shipment of arms to Croat depots via Hungary. The revelation heightened fears that Croatia was about to break away from the rest of the Federation. An independence referendum was then held on May 2, 1991, with 93% of voters opting for autonomy. Tudjman subsequently declared independence

---

[65] Tom Buchanan, *Europe's Troubled Peace. 1945 to the Present* (Chichester: Wiley-Blackwell, 2012, 2nd ed), p. 242.

[66] John R. Lampe, *Yugoslavia as History. Twice there was a country* (Cambridge: Cambridge University Press, 2000), p. 332.

on June 25, the same day as the Slovenes.

While Slovenia successfully left after a short war, Croatia would face a much tougher departure. In fact, Croatia would be at war for over four years. Milošević's argument to the Croats was that the principle of self-determination should apply to Serbs in the country, therefore giving them the option to separate from the rest of Croatia. This was obviously anathema to the Croat leadership.

There were some large regions of majority-Serb populations. One was the Krajina, which included Knin and bordered Serb-dominated parts of Bosnia and Herzegovina. The others were Western Slavonia and Eastern Slavonia, in the northeast of Croatia and bordering Serbia. All three areas were backed by Serbia, supplied with weapons and diplomatic support. They soon declared themselves autonomous regions, outside the sovereignty of any Croat state.

Fighting had broken out between Serbs and Croats in Plitvice in April 1991, an area of conjoining lakes popular among tourists, but this low-level conflict expanded into a full-scale war. Nominally protecting Serbs in the autonomous regions, the JNA moved on the major coastal Croatian cities of Split and Dubrovnik in the summer of 1991 after the independence declaration.[67] By shelling these cities indiscriminately, the JNA was besieging the Croats and terrorizing their populations, attempting to extort political concessions from Zagreb. At the time, the JNA claimed it was targeting Ustaše terrorists in both cities.

Following this initial reasoning, the Serbs and their allies the Montenegrins set their sights on capturing the ancient city of Dubrovnik. Both Split and Dubrovnik were hugely popular with Western tourists. The latter was dubbed the "Pearl of the Adriatic," and therefore a significant source of foreign currency for Croatia. The sieges hit the fledgling Croatian state financially and in terms of prestige, and the fighting caused cultural vandalism in the process. This latter point was probably important in the swift international condemnation that was aimed at Belgrade and the Yugoslav leadership from the international community.

Shortly after Slovenia and Croatia declared independence in June 1991 and fighting erupted, the United Nations and European Community sought to intervene diplomatically. The Europeans, shocked by the first major violence on the continent in years, scrambled to respond. Aware that the United States wanted to quell the violence, the Europeans took center stage instead. Confident after the fall of the Berlin Wall, and with the Community about to expand into the European Union, one foreign minister, Jacques Poos, hubristically proclaimed the "Hour of Europe" had come. As a result, the European Community deployed negotiators, former British Foreign Secretary Lord Carrington and Portuguese diplomat José Cutileiro, to reach a diplomatic solution.[68]

---

[67] Chuck Sudetic, 'Shelling of Besieged Yugoslav Port Is Intensified', *The New York Times*, 13 November 1991, https://www.nytimes.com/1991/11/13/world/shelling-of-besieged-yugoslav-port-is-intensified.html, [accessed 31 October 2018]

The conflict in Croatia soon developed an internal Hobbesian logic. Although a federal Yugoslavia still nominally existed, when Slovenia and Croatia declared independence, Belgrade, the JNA, and the Federation basically came to resemble nothing more than a rump state of Serbia. As the JNA moved in to prevent Slovenia and Croatia from leaving the Federation, and also to protect Serbs in Krajina and Slavonia, the mandate appeared to shift. The longer the fighting dragged on, the more it looked as if the JNA was an agent for Serb domination and even conquest.

As Dubrovnik remained under siege, the JNA turned its attention to the Croatian city of Vukovar. With a mixed population of Serbs and Croats, Vukovar lay to the east of Croatia, within the Serb-declared region of Eastern Slavonia. After the declaration of Serb Krajina earlier in 1991, Vukovar became a focal point for tension between Serbs and Croats in the region. Barricades were erected, militias formed, and fighting broke out between groups soon afterwards. The Croat authorities sent forces of under 2,000 to defend the city from a JNA or Serb militia takeover. After the declaration of independence by Zagreb, fighting in and around Vukovar worsened and the JNA did indeed surround the city. From early October 1991, the JNA besieged Vukovar, pummelling it with shells and attempting to starve its inhabitants into submission. The Croat forces defending the city launched offensives against the JNA but were hopelessly outnumbered. JNA troops numbered 36,000, an overwhelming advantage.

The JNA launched their own offensive in November 1991 and took control of the city from the Croats. What followed was chilling, and a harbinger for later events in Bosnia and Herzegovina. In their acclaimed book, *The Death of Yugoslavia*, authors Laura Silber and Allan Little described the aftermath of the Battle of Vukovar as a horrific scene of corpses, chaos and destruction.[69] The Croat population of around 20,000 was forced to leave the city, their homes were looted, and a number of massacres and rapes were carried out by the attacking forces. Many Croats were taken prisoner and detained. Vukovar and its aftermath set the pattern for much of the subsequent fighting, and the city itself would be part of the self-proclaimed Serb Krajina republic until 1995, when Croats retook control of Vukovar.

The negotiators finally brought pressure to bear on the Yugoslavs and the JNA at the end of 1991. A ceasefire was declared in January 1992, and the UN deployed peacekeepers as part of its UN Protection Force (UNPROFOR). The UN "Blue Helmets" were mandated to protect the population in three areas, called "Safe Havens." As a result, the conflict in Croatia was frozen until the summer of 1995.

The UN and its Security Council had been dormant for much of the Cold War, but now that the

---

[68] Alan Riding, 'Conflict in Yugoslavia; Europeans send high-level team', *The New York Times*, 29 June 1991, https://www.nytimes.com/1991/06/29/world/conflict-in-yugoslavia-europeans-send-high-level-team.html, [accessed 31 October 2018]

[69] Laura Silber and Allan Little, *The Death of Yugoslavia* (London: Penguin, 1996), p. 180.

superpower confrontation was over, more decisions could be passed without a veto. The early 1990s were a period when the West, now led by a sole superpower, could attempt to mold the international landscape in its image. The UN wanted to enforce international law, self-determination, and human rights standards in Yugoslavia, but there was no consensus on the best approach in the Balkans after 1991. Events in the region threw up devilishly complex challenges where liberal principles contradicted each other. After all, how could national self-determination be applied in ethnically and nationally mixed societies? What was an appropriate use of external force to restore order and prevent further violence? How could minority rights be secured in the successor states? These issues would be hotly debated over the course of the 1990s and only reach some kind of consensus by the time of the Kosovo crisis in 1998-1999.

The Bosnian War

Much has been written about Western intervention during the breakup of Yugoslavia, and whether it made matters worse, prevented worse atrocities, or was simply ineffective. In early 1992, however, what was clear was that Europe was hopelessly divided over the best course of action to take towards Yugoslavia.

On January 15, 1992, most European countries recognized the independence of Slovenia and Croatia. The matter had caused bitter division between the major European powers. The newly-reunified Germany was the most enthusiastic backer of Slovene and Croat independence, partly for historical reasons and partly due to its huge expatriate community of Croats. France and Britain, however, were opposed, as both countries were traditionally more pro-Serb and were by the early 1990s wary of an expanded Germany throwing its weight around diplomatically.[70] Against European Community protocol, German Foreign Minister Hans Dietrich Genscher unilaterally recognized the two states at the end of 1991, therefore compelling most of the rest of the Community to do likewise a few weeks later.[71] Britain and France were concerned that recognition would set a dangerous precedent and encourage similar actions – and military conflicts – by the competing groups in Bosnia and Herzegovina, as well as alienating the region's largest group, the Serbs.

The role of the United States was more ambiguous.[72] Some accounts of the period have suggested that the US Ambassador in Belgrade, Warren Zimmermann, was strongly in favor of independence for the republics, while others have stated that America had little interest in the Balkan region with so many other foreign challenges taking place, notably the Gulf War and the collapse of the Soviet Union.

On February 29 and March 1 in 1992, Bosnia and Herzegovina held an independence referendum. With a turnout of 63%, almost all respondents voted for independence. Crucially,

[70] Vesna Drapac, *Constructing Yugoslavia: A Transnational History*, (Basingstoke: Palgrave Macmillan, 2010), p. 255.
[71] Tom Buchanan, *Europe's Troubled Peace, 1945 to the Present* (Chichester: Wiley-Blackwell, 2012, 2nd ed p. 243.
[72] Alastair Finlan, *The Collapse of Yugoslavia 1991-1999*, (Oxford: Osprey, 2004), p. 44.

many Bosnian Serbs boycotted the poll, but shortly afterwards, the country's leader, Alija Izetbegović, declared independence.

Izetbegović

By this point, it was surely clear to the Sarajevo leadership that autonomy would be fraught with difficulty. If Slovenia was a more straightforward proposition than Croatia, then Croatia was less hazardous than Bosnia and Herzegovina. A remnant of the Ottoman Empire, Bosnia had been hailed as recently as the 1984 Sarajevo Winter Olympic Games as a triumph of Yugoslav multiethnic harmony. Wedged in the middle of Yugoslavia, Bosnia and Herzegovina bordered Croatia, Serbia, and Montenegro, and it was divided between Bosniaks (44%), Bosnian Serbs (33%) and Bosnian Croats (17%). The Serbs, who were mainly Orthodox Christians, lived predominantly in the border areas to the east, while the Croats, mainly Catholic, lived in the West. The Bosniaks, who were mainly Muslims, lived in the central parts, including the capital, Sarajevo.

Tensions increased in Bosnia and Herzegovina after Slovenia and Croatia's declarations of independence in June 1991. In some respects, Izetbegović was pushed towards independence hastily and even against his reservations. Nevertheless, it seemed a window had opened, and Bosnia would need to leave Yugoslavia to avoid the tyranny of Milošević.

Bosnian Serbs were also worried that they, like their brethren in Croatia, would be cut adrift from the Federation (and the main Serb Republic) if they were incorporated into a Bosnian state. Preempting a possible move to independence by Sarajevo, the Bosnian Serbs, led by Radovan Karadžić, called a referendum in November 1991, which resulted in a large majority in favor of staying part of Serbia or Yugoslavia. At the beginning of 1992, Karadžić declared the Bosnian Serb Republic in a similar fashion to Serb Krajina in Croatia.

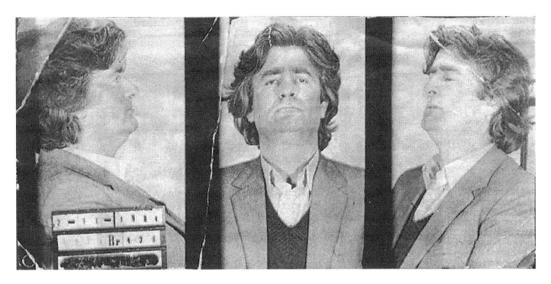

Karadžić

The European negotiators, aware that Bosnia was rapidly becoming a tinderbox, turned their attention to the republic. In March 1992, Carrington and Cutileiro presented a peace plan for Bosnia and Herzegovina, essentially dividing the country into semi-autonomous cantons based on each locality's majority group.[73] The executive and various levels of government and administration would be based upon power-sharing. All three groups accepted the plan on March 18, 1992, with Izetbegović for the Bosniaks, Karadžić for the Serbs, and Mate Boban for the Croats. Izetbegović, however, inexplicably withdrew his support 10 days later following a meeting with Zimmermann in Belgrade. It may be that Izetbegović believed he had been given an assurance of American support for a separate, presumably Bosniak-led version of the state, but regardless, it turned out to be a fateful decision. After the withdrawal, all three groups temporarily retreated, and many of the more hardline factions prepared for the kind of war that had erupted in Croatia the previous year.

The start of hostilities in Bosnia and Herzegovina has been disputed. One account was that the Bosniaks opened fire on a Serb wedding on March 1, while Silber and Little state that the Serb shooting into a crowd of civilians in Sarajevo on April 5 commenced hostilities. What is clear is that after these events, Bosnia and Herzegovina descended into a war more horrific than anything

---

[73] Josip Glaurdić, *The Hour of Europe: Western Powers and the Breakup of Yugoslavia* (London: Yale University Press, 2011), p. 294.

that had occurred since 1945. Apart from the thousands of deaths from fighting between armies and militias, the targeting of civilians was common, especially during the siege of Sarajevo that lasted about three-and-a-half-years. As had been seen in Vukovar in 1991, many people were forced from their homes, held in concentration camps, and even executed on account of their ethnicity. The grim term "ethnic cleansing" moved into the public consciousness during this time.[74]

The politicians had failed to reach a diplomatic agreement in Bosnia and Herzegovina, and one of the great tragedies of the Bosnian example would be that the eventual peace agreement signed in November 1995 would look remarkably similar to the plan rejected in March 1992. Now it was the turn of the military commanders, militia leaders, and a variety of hardliners and extreme nationalists to settle the numerous disputes through force of arms.

Unfortunately for the Bosniaks in particular, it was the JNA which had the majority of the arms, and they were mostly pro-Serb. JNA positions used the hills around Sarajevo to bombard the city daily with artillery fire and cut off supplies. Serb forces made gains around the country throughout 1992 and wasted no time in revealing their malevolent tactics. Serbs took a brutal approach toward civilians in Banja Luka and Srebrenica, and Bosnian President Izetbegović was even taken hostage in May 1992 as he returned to Sarajevo from its airport before being freed after negotiations.[75]

Meanwhile, the international community, especially Britain and France, reinforced the arms embargo to Yugoslavia that had been in place since the previous year. Since the JNA already had a large repository of weapons, the effect of the embargo in practice was to leave the Bosniaks and Bosnian Croats hopelessly exposed to Serb aggression. For its part, UNPROFOR expanded its mission into Bosnia, also setting up safe havens in Srebrenica, Žepa, Goražde, Tuzla and Bihać.

It was soon clear that the violence in Bosnia and Herzegovina would eclipse that in Croatia the previous year. The ferocity of the ethnic killings, the disregard for civilians, the disdain for human rights, the aggression of the propaganda, and the use of concentration camps was wholly different than what had come before it in Yugoslavia's breakup, and once the fighting started in Bosnia, forces were unleashed that were extremely difficult to contain. Whether it was "ancient hatreds" as many commentators believed, wartime memories, or the insecurity and anarchical conditions of the period, the almost immediate brutality on show in Bosnia shocked the world. The early 1990s was a period when 24-hour news channels and satellite television networks came into being, ensuring that the Yugoslav Wars and its grisly footage would be broadcast into people's homes across the world almost daily for four years. After the optimism generated by the

[74] Christopher Bennett, *Yugoslavia's Bloody Collapse. Causes, Course and Consequences* (London: Hurst & Company, 1998), p. 238.
[75] Dan Damon, 'When my father was taken captive in Sarajevo', BBC News, 2 May 2012, https://www.bbc.com/news/world-europe-17913518, [accessed 1 November 2018]

end of the Cold War, it was clear that this sense of hope was not shared even throughout Europe. Many observers, journalists, politicians and members of the public decried the inability of governments or the much-vaunted "international community" to do anything about the carnage. That would continue when other atrocities took place during the decade, such as the 1994 Rwandan genocide.

A picture of damage done during the Bosnian War

A picture of damage done during the Siege of Sarajevo

UN Blue Helmets near Sarajevo

The UN increased its role in 1992. In addition to the work of UNPROFOR, the UN authorized a negotiator, former US Secretary of State Cyrus Vance, to work with the newly appointed European negotiator, former British Foreign Secretary David Owen.[76] Both the blue helmets and the negotiators, however, proved ineffective in their objectives. The UN forces were, understandably, supposed to be neutral, and mandated to protect civilians rather than intervene in the fighting. This became a highly difficult task, given that the combatants only had intermittent respect for the neutral position of the UN forces. Occasionally, they even engaged the UN forces.

The negotiators, meanwhile, undertook shuttle diplomacy between Sarajevo and Belgrade, as well as other European capitals and locations in Yugoslavia, in a fruitless attempt to stop the fighting and find a diplomatic solution. They produced a number of peace plans which essentially developed the Carrington-Cutileiro idea further. The Vance-Owen Peace Plan (VOPP) was unveiled in January 1993, proposing the cantons form three separate provinces with Sarajevo having a special status. A successor plan, the Owen-Stoltenberg Plan, produced with Vance's replacement Thorvald Stoltenberg, a Norwegian diplomat, further established these principles.

The problem with the plans was not their formulation, which set out the basis of the eventual peace agreement. Simply put, in 1992 and 1993, the Bosnian Serbs were winning the conflict. With the support of the JNA and Belgrade, and with the arms embargo crippling the Bosniaks, there was no incentive for the Serbs, or Milošević, to compromise. Serb nationalists such as Karadžić could pursue goals of an ethnically homogeneous Greater Serbia, made up of Serbia, the Bosnian Serb areas, Serb Krajina, and Montenegro.

Yugoslav Prime Minister Ante Marković had been forced from an office that essentially no longer existed as Slovenia and Croatia left the Federation. Much later, Marković testified about those final days of Yugoslavia, stating that he was aware of an arrangement made between Slobodan Milošević and Franjo Tudjman in March 1991 at Karađorđevo in Vojvodina to divide up Bosnia and Herzegovina along their own ethnic lines. This alleged agreement has been vigorously denied in the years since, but the Croats would soon enter the fighting.

In 1992, the majority of the fighting in Bosnia took place between the JNA-backed Bosnian Serbs and the rearguard action of the Bosniaks. By the end of the year, Serbs controlled almost 67% of the entire country. As the fighting dragged on into 1993, Bosnian Croats also attacked the Bosniaks. The Sarajevo authorities were now desperately defending their fledgling state from two sides.

Herzegovina was home to many Croats, and in the middle of the ostensibly Bosniak-Serb war, the Croats attempted to set up their own enclave, the "Republic of Herzeg-Bosnia." Similar areas were now dotted across the former Yugoslavia, where the ethnic minority in that country formed an outpost in which its particular group was in the majority, such as Serb Krajina, Slavonia, and

---

[76] David Owen, *Balkan Odyssey* (London: Indigo, 1996)

the Bosnian Serb entity dubbed Republika Srpska (Serb Republic).

Fighting broke out between Bosniaks and Croats, often in a brutal fashion. The Croats made initial gains as the Bosniaks lost more and more territory, impeded as they were by a lack of arms. One visible symbol of this conflict was the destruction of the Stari Most bridge across the Neretva River in the mixed city of Mostar. As fighting escalated, each side took up positions on either side of the bridge until November 9, 1993, when Croat artillery shelled and destroyed the Stari Most. The bridge, an architectural masterpiece, had stood for 427 years.

Josephine W. Baker's picture of the bridge in the 1970s

Eventually, the Bosnian army pushed back Croat forces. Receiving material support from a number of Islamic countries, notably Iran and Pakistan, as well as volunteers, the Bosniaks managed to turn the tide somewhat after their initial setbacks. Partly as a result of this new reality, the Clinton administration pressured the Bosnian Croats to join forces with the Bosniaks in March 1994 as part of the Washington Agreement. The Croat-Bosniak fighting thus ended and the joint Federation of Bosnia and Herzegovina was formed.

Even after they were done fighting each other, Federation forces faced bad odds against the

Serb army. Sarajevo was under constant artillery shelling while snipers around the city would shoot civilians attempting to go about daily life, such as it still existed. A number of particularly horrific bombs destroyed parts of Sarajevo and shocked the outside world, including several marketplace bombs.[77] On August 30, 1992 a Sarajevo marketplace was bombed by a Serb shell, killing 15, and on February 5, 1994, the Markale marketplace was attacked, killing 66.[78]

After each atrocity, international opinion was stirred and hardened against the Serbs. Apart from terrorizing the besieged population, bombing civilians had no strategic purpose and worked as negative propaganda against the Bosnian Serbs, as well as Slobodan Milošević, by now President of Serbia.

The Bosnian War had been raging for three years by the summer of 1995, and UN and European negotiators had tried in vain to bring the various sides to a diplomatic solution. Milošević and Karadžić had proven masters in deception and ambiguity. By that August, the negotiators had all but given up. Whether the Serbs knew the conflict would soon reach a climax is difficult to know, but they embarked upon a course that would finally turn international opinion decisively against them and draw a severe military and diplomatic response from the United States. President Clinton's administration had been infuriated by events in Yugoslavia, and they were disgusted with the leaders on all sides and the UN and European negotiators.

Reports began to emerge about a massacre in the eastern Bosnian town of Srebrenica in July 1995. Home to a large number of Bosnian Muslims, Srebrenica had been delegated a "safe haven" and protected as such by UN blue helmet peacekeepers. The reasons for what happened next is hotly disputed, but Bosnian Serb forces, commanded by General Ratko Mladić, overran the town and peacekeepers, expelling many of the Bosniaks there and leading around 8,000 men and boys into the surrounding countryside to be executed. The Srebrenica massacre was the worst war crime to take place in Europe in 50 years, and it provided ample evidence of a campaign of genocide by the Serbs against the Bosnian Muslims.

---

[77] Bill Clinton, *My Life* (London: Arrow, 2005), p. 581.

[78] John Kifner, '66 Die as Shell Wrecks Sarajevo Market', *The New York Times* 6 February 1994, https://www.nytimes.com/1994/02/06/world/66-die-as-shell-wrecks-sarajevo-market.html, [accessed 1 November 2018]

A picture of massacre victims being exhumed

Mladić

When news of the massacre reached the outside world (Dutch UNPROFOR peacekeepers had been forced to step aside as the victims were taken prisoner), the calls for something to be done reached a fevered pitch. Then, on August 28, 1995, Serb artillery shells hit the Markale marketplace yet again, this time killing 43. This was the final straw for the Clinton administration. A NATO force, Operation Deliberate Force, bombed Bosnian Serb positions in an effort to stop the shelling of civilian areas, including safe havens. The raids led to the deaths of 27 Bosnian Serb soldiers and the same number of Bosnian Serb civilians.

Shortly before the NATO strikes, the Clinton administration approved a secret Croatian offensive to take back the Serb enclaves within its territory. The Croatian armed forces, which had been preparing the operation for some time, were keen to exploit the increased anti-Serb sentiment in the international media, and they overwhelmed the makeshift Serb defences across Krajina. In a matter of days, Croats were in control of their entire territory.

The fates of the Croatian Serbs, however, were grim. Virtually all were forced from their homes and effectively displaced, vilified as a "fifth column" within Croatia. Around 200,000 Croatian Serbs – whose lineage there went back centuries - were displaced and turned into refugees, forced to trudge to the Republika Srpska or Serbia itself. This was another example of ethnic cleansing, albeit a less violent one.

Further NATO airstrikes in late September 1995 put further pressure on the Serbs. By November that year the Serb leadership was on the backfoot after years of obstinence in the face of international condemnation. The leaders of the three main Bosnian nationalities were summoned to the American airbase in Dayton, Ohio in November. Alija Izetbegović, representing the Bosniaks, Franjo Tudjman, representing the Croats, and Slobodan Milošević, representing the Serbs (it was noteworthy that Radovan Karadžić did not travel to Dayton), argued relentlessly, but finally, under pressure and threats from the Clinton administration, they signed a peace treaty.[79]

The Dayton Accords were similar to the previous peace plans set forth by Carrington, Cutileiro, Owen, Vance and Stoltenberg. They ostensibly allowed division in Bosnia and Herzegovina along federal lines, with a Bosniak-Croatian Federation – based at Sarajevo - governing 51% of the country, and a Republika Srpska – based at Banja Luka - controlling the remaining 49%. All levels of government and administration throughout the country would be based upon the principles of power-sharing.

The fighting had ended at the cost of some 250,000 dead and two million people displaced.[80] The wounds of the conflict, however, would take much longer to heal. A better description of the Dayton Accords might have been that they froze the conflict. The Serbs had, more or less, been rewarded for their territorial gains. The Republika Srpska would develop into a nationalistic enterprise whose leadership continues to agitate for independence from the Federation.

---

[79] Bill Clinton, *My Life* (London: Arrow, 2005), pp. 684-685.
[80] Bill Clinton, *My Life* (London: Arrow, 2005), p. 684.

The Bitter End

Yugoslavia was long dead by the time of the Dayton Accords. Bosnia and Herzegovina, Croatia, and Slovenia had all left with varying degrees of difficulty. Macedonia had also declared independence, recognized in 1992, with minimal fuss despite its own mixed population. After Dayton, the name Yugoslavia endured, but now it only included Serbia, Vojvodina, Montenegro and Kosovo.

To the outside world, Milošević – as well as Bosnian Serb leaders such as Ratko Mladic and Radovan Karadžić – appeared most accountable for the carnage of the 1990s in the Balkans. The Serbs may have complained that this was unfair, a simplification of hugely complex forces and events, and indeed, Croatian Serbs had suffered grievously at the end of the conflict. Still, many in the international community concluded that the main culprits in the wars were the Serbs. It didn't help the Serbs that their traditional ally, Russia (which shared Orthodox Christianity with the Serbs), was in crisis and retreat -

Milošević, of course, had drawn a different conclusion. Despite sanctions and international condemnation, Milošević was still in power and essentially presiding over a Greater Serbia, albeit a smaller one than it might've included with sovereignty over Serbian enclaves in Croatia and Bosnia. He personally had not been implicated in any atrocity or war crimes - in fact, he was welcomed in foreign capitals as a peacekeeper, signing peace treaties. It may be that Milošević, who was later deeply implicated in the horrors of the conflicts, felt a sense of impunity. After all, despite the opprobrium directed at the Bosnian Serbs, a policy of territorial conquest and ethnic cleansing had at least partially paid dividends.

It was against this backdrop that the final major act in the history of Yugoslavia played out in Kosovo.

Croat nationalists had sought independence for much of the Federation's existence. Bosnia and Herzegovina had much less of a tradition of separatism, but both were excruciatingly divided from Yugoslavia due to large Serb minorities who opposed separation or wanted their own separate status. Kosovo, however, was a different topic altogether. The province was considered an integral part of Serbia, crucial to understanding the Serb nation and its defining moment of awakening on the battlefield in 1389. Slobodan Milošević had exploited this strong nationalist attachment during his speech there on the occasion of the battle's 600th anniversary in June 1989.

The reality of life in 20th century Kosovo, however, was somewhat detached from these romantic notions. Kosovo was 90% ethnic Albanian, with only a tiny minority of Serbs. Tensions had increased after Tito's death in 1980, and Kosovar Albanians had demonstrated in 1981, seeking greater cultural recognition. On the other side, Serbs had protested in 1987 over alleged discrimination and police prejudice.[81] The latter episode had led to Milošević's trip there and his subsequent positioning as defender of the Serbs. Milošević had subsequently installed his own supporters in positions of authority in Kosovo, apparently dampening the disturbances.

In the late 1980s and much of the 1990s, Kosovo was experiencing a cold peace, but Kosovar Albanians dreamed of their own imperial project, Greater Albania, which would include Albania, Kosovo, and parts of Macedonia. They perceived that their moment might be approaching after the four republics had left Yugoslavia and life under Milošević's rule would surely not be pleasant for Albanians in Kosovo, particularly after the Serb strongman had forged his reputation on the ethnic issue.

In 1991, the Kosovo Liberation Army (KLA) was formed. Styled more on an outdated Cold War model of national independence through armed tactics, mainly of the guerrilla variety, the KLA presented a different challenge than the political movements of Slovenia, Croatia, and Bosnia and Herzegovina. The KLA began to target Serb police and government installations, as well as civilians, in 1995.[82] Throughout this time, weapons and equipment were smuggled to the guerrillas via Albania.

Certainly, the ethnic Albanian population had suffered oppression, especially after Milošević had come to power, but at a different time, the KLA would probably have been portrayed as an illegal, violent group which the government was attempting to defeat. The previous carnage in the region changed all that, and with the Serbs being blamed for the violence, the KLA was viewed somewhat sympathetically. Moreover, Western politicians were anxious to prevent a replay of those conflicts in Kosovo.

A campaign of sabotage increased in 1997, while ethnic tensions simmered between Kosovar Serbs and Albanians. The pattern worsened that year as a result of events in neighboring Albania. The loss of authority in March 1997 of Albanian President Berisha led to military repositories and arsenals being looted, meaning the country was suddenly awash with weapons. As anarchy descended on Albania, many of these weapons found their way into the hands of the KLA. Then, in a pattern reminiscent of the conflicts in Croatia and Bosnia, as the minority Serbs became fearful of the majority, many took matters into their hands.

Naturally, Milošević promised to defend the Serb population at any cost. In March 1998, the Yugoslav army again intervened, attacking KLA positions. The violence escalated over the next year, and a familiar pattern of ethnic cleansing, looting, and displacement all played out. Everything was covered once more by the international media, and when scenes of refugees and ethnic Albanians desperately fleeing Serb aggression reached a global audience, the West decided to act.

---

[81] Laura Silber and Allan Little, *The Death of Yugoslavia* (London: Penguin, 1995)
[82] Peter Beaumont, 'KLA goes on killing rampage', *The Guardian*, 27 June 1999,
   https://www.theguardian.com/world/1999/jun/27/balkans2, [accessed 1 November 2018]

Western politicians were desperate not to watch a repeat of the fighting in Bosnia, and the Clinton administration had been scarred by events involving American forces in Somalia. Throughout the rest of his time in office, military action consisted almost solely of airstrikes. The high-tech US Air Force force was praised for its precision bombing ability, and importantly for Clinton, this approach avoided American casualties.

A NATO summit was held in the French castle of Rambouillet in January 1999, and Milošević was put on notice that if he did not end the campaign of ethnic cleansing, NATO would be forced to intervene. Not satisfied with the response but unable to secure a UN Security Council Resolution on the matter (by 1999, Russia had regained enough composure to offer Serbia its support), NATO launched an air campaign in March 1999. The air strikes lasted for several months, without the desired effect of forcing a withdrawal. In fact, on May 7, NATO bombs hit the Chinese embassy in Belgrade, killing three and causing an international incident.[83]

British Prime Minister Tony Blair, who had then been in office for less than two years, took a keen interest in the conflict. The previous wars had convinced Blair that the West had a moral duty to intervene when it could to prevent human rights abuses. Blair would pursue his principle of humanitarian intervention in Kosovo. The key to success, Blair believed, was to pose the threat of an American-led ground invasion. Once that was credibly on the table, then Milošević would back down.

Clinton and Tony Blair were close allies but very nearly fell out over this matter. Clinton was opposed to the use of American soldiers to back up any threat. In the end, however, Blair convinced the American president, and once a ground invasion was set in motion. In response, the army was indeed quickly withdrawn by Milošević, and the Kosovo War was over by the middle of June 1999.

The outcome was similar to what took place in Bosnia and Herzegovina. A UN Protectorate was established in Kosovo, which lasted until 2008, when the Kosovar authorities declared independence, much to the outrage of Belgrade. For all intents and purposes, the conflict in Kosovo, like Bosnia, is still frozen. Tony Blair would go on to consider the Kosovo intervention a defining success, and it would guide his policies, most notably his support for the 2003 Iraq invasion.

Kosovo was the final straw for Yugoslavia's viability. The violence that had gripped Kosovo spilled over the border with Macedonia, where a latent conflict almost took hold between Macedonians and ethnic Albanians. This time, however, international negotiators entered the fray effectively. Under the auspices of NATO, the "Ohrid Agreement" was signed in August 2001 as a means of adapting the Macedonian constitution to ensure Albanian rights.

---

[83] Steven Lee Meyers, 'Chinese Embassy Bombing: A Wide Net of Blame', *The New York Times*, 17 April 2000, https://www.nytimes.com/2000/04/17/world/chinese-embassy-bombing-a-wide-net-of-blame.html, [accessed 1 November 2018]

By this time, Milošević had finally been removed from office. After the 1999 Kosovo War, he was indicted by the International Criminal Tribunal for the former Yugoslavia in the Hague for war crimes there, as well as in Bosnia and Croatia. Milošević refused to surrender himself and stood for reelection in 2000. When it appeared that the results had been fixed by Milošević, crowds took to the streets of Belgrade demanding he step down, which he finally did on October 6, 2000. A few months later, Yugoslav authorities handed Milošević over to the Hague tribunal. Although he stood trial, Milošević never received a sentence due to dying in prison of a heart attack in 2006. His former mentor and rival, Ivan Stambolić, was assassinated in 2000. After an inquest by the authorities, Milošević was found to have arranged a mafia-style "hit."[84]

Yugoslavia formally folded in 2006 after Montenegrins voted in a referendum to leave the Federation, though in reality, Yugoslavia had not truly existed for several years. Today, the states of the former Yugoslavia are either EU members or candidates. The latter face huge challenges to fulfill this ambition. Apart from the often authoritarian and corrupt political systems in place, these states need to resolve outstanding territorial claims before they can achieve membership. Needless to say, the hangover caused by the disintegration of Yugoslavia has turned out to be long and painful.

The demise of Yugoslavia disconcerted Western society and led to much soul-searching after the fact. Many wondered how a country that seemed financially successful for long stretches could come apart at the seams so quickly and spectacularly. But as any examination of the complete history of the state demonstrates, it faced significant challenges from its very inception. Perhaps the story of Yugoslavia should focus more on how the multinational state survived as long as it did.

Online Resources

Other books about 20th century history by Charles River Editors

Other books about Tito on Amazon

Bibliography

Badredine Arfi, *International Change and the Stability of Multiethnic States. Yugoslavia, Lebanon, and Crises of Governance.* (Indianapolis: Indiana University Press, 2005)

David Binder, 'A Coffin for Mihailovic', *New York Times*, 10 February 1991, https://www.nytimes.com/1991/02/10/books/a-coffin-for-mihailovic.html

Nada Boskovska, *Yugoslavia and Macedonia Before Tito: Between Repression and Integration*

---

[84] Vesna Peric Zimonjic, 'Death squad leader guilty of killing Serbian president', *The Independent,* 19 July 2005, https://www.independent.co.uk/news/world/europe/death-squad-leader-guilty-of-killing-serbian-president-300063.html, [accessed 1 November 2018]

(London: IB Tauris, 2016)

Christopher Catherwood, *Churchill and Tito: SOE, Bletchley Park and Supporting the Yugoslav Communists in World War II* (Frontline Books, 2017)

Dejan Djokić, 'Versailles and Yugoslavia: ninety years on', *Open Democracy*, 26 June 2009, https://www.opendemocracy.net/article/versailles-and-yugoslavia-ninety-years-on

Dejan Djokić, *Pasic & Trumbic: The Kingdom of Serbs, Croats and Slovenes*. (Haus Publishing, 2010)

Vesna Drapac, *Constructing Yugoslavia: A Transnational History*, (Basingstoke: Palgrave Macmillan, 2010)

Richard J. Evans, *The Pursuit of Power: Europe 1815-1914* (London: Penguin, 2017)

Tom Gallagher, *Outcast Europe: The Balkans, 1789-1989: From the Ottomans to Milošević*, (London: Routledge, 2001)

Robert Gerwarth, *The Vanquished: Why the First World War Failed to End, 1917-1923* (London: Allen Lane, 2016)

Ivo Goldstein, 'The Independent State of Croatia in 1941: On the Road to Catastrophe', *Totalitarian Movements and Political Religions*, 7:4, 2006, pp. 417-427

Misha Glenny, *The Balkans 1804-2012: Nationalism, War and the Great Powers* (London: Granta, 2012)

The History Channel, '1941: Yugoslavia joins the Axis', (A&E Networks, 2009), https://www.history.com/this-day-in-history/yugoslavia-joins-the-axis

Godfrey Hodgson, *People's Century: From the dawn of the century to the eve of the millennium* (Godalming: BBC Books, 1998)

Paul Kennedy, *The Rise and Fall of the Great Powers: Economic Change and Military Conflict from 1500 to 2000* (New York: Random House, 1987)

James M. Lindsay, 'TWE Remembers: Austria-Hungary Issues an Ultimatum to Serbia', *Council on Foreign Relations*, 23 July 2014, https://www.cfr.org/blog/twe-remembers-austria-hungary-issues-ultimatum-serbia

Sonia Lucarelli, *Europe and the Breakup of Yugoslavia. A Political Failure in Search of a Scholarly Explanation*, (The Hague: Kluwer Law International, 2000)

Oto Luthar (ed), *The Land Between: A History of Slovenia* (Frankfurt am Main: Peter Lang, 2008)

Blanka Matkovich, *Croatia and Slovenia at the End and After the Second World War (1944-1945): Mass Crimes and Human Rights Violations Committed by the Communist Regime*, (Brown Walker Press, 2017)

Mark Mazower, *The Balkans: From the End of Byzantium to the Present Day* (London: Phoenix, 2001)

Eugene Michail, 'Western Attitudes to War in the Balkans and the Shifting Meanings of Violence, 1912-1991', *Journal of Contemporary History*, (47:219, 2012), 219-241.

Eugene Michail, *The British and the Balkans. Forming Images of Foreign Lands, 1900-1950.* (London: Continuum, 2011)

David Owen, *Balkan Odyssey* (London: Indigo, 1996)

Laura Silber and Allan Little, *The Death of Yugoslavia* (London: Penguin, 1996)

Brendan Simms, *Europe: The Struggle for Supremacy 1453 to the Present* (London: Penguin, 2014)

Brendan Simms, *Unfinest Hour: Britain and the Destruction of Bosnia*, (London: Penguin, 2001)

Free Books by Charles River Editors

We have brand new titles available for free most days of the week. To see which of our titles are currently free, click on this link.

Discounted Books by Charles River Editors

We have titles at a discount price of just 99 cents everyday. To see which of our titles are currently 99 cents, click on this link.

Made in the USA
Columbia, SC
26 May 2023

17346897R00041